Relax and Color
Scripture in Flowers

ISBN: 978-1-7358328-5-2

Finch Hollow Press LLC 2023

Color Swatches

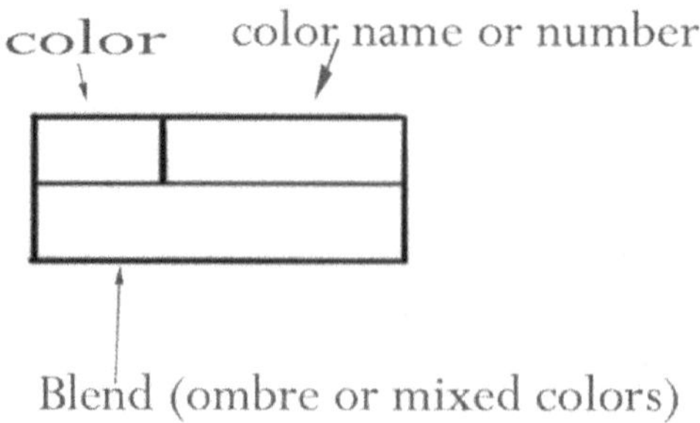

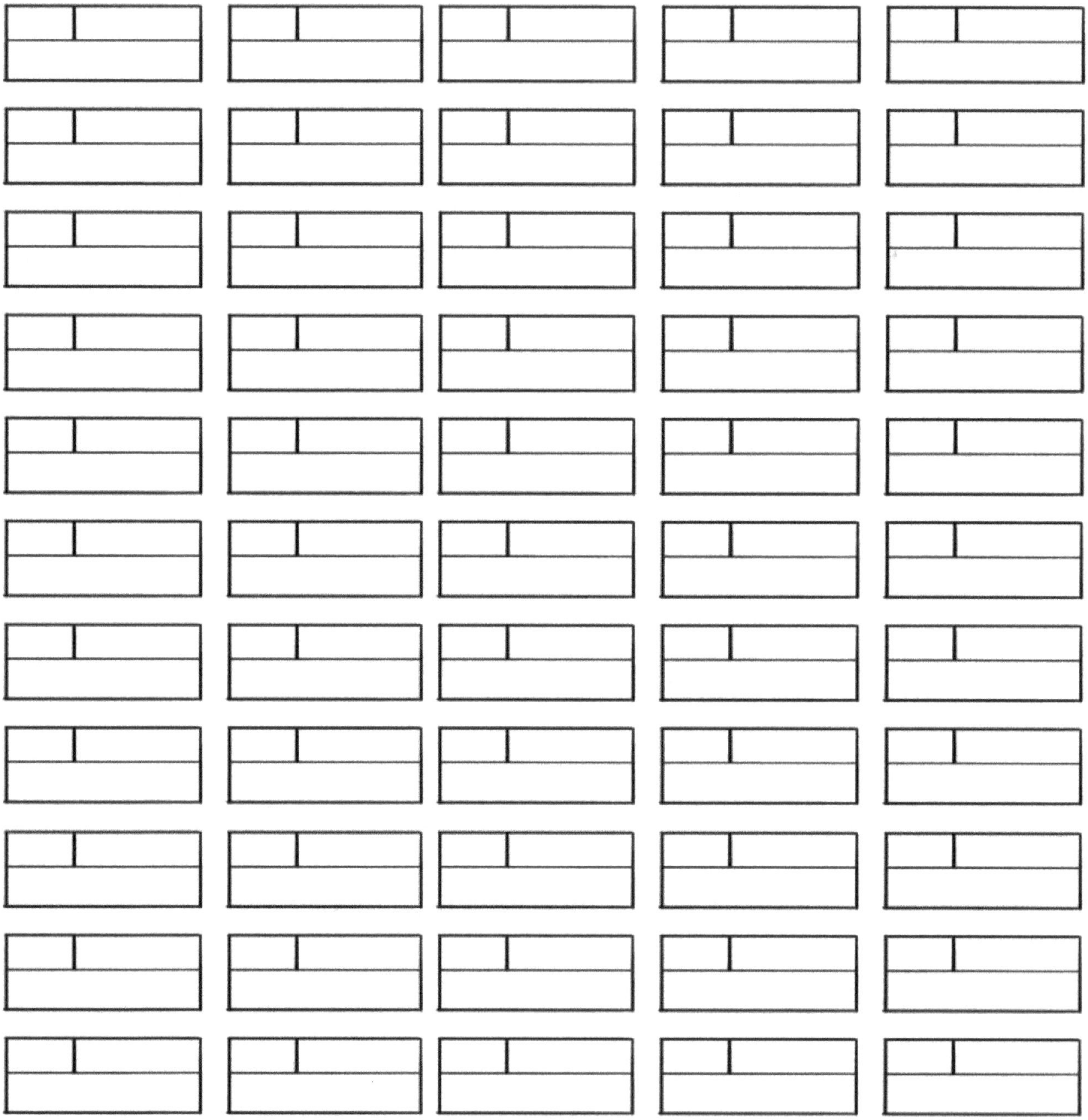

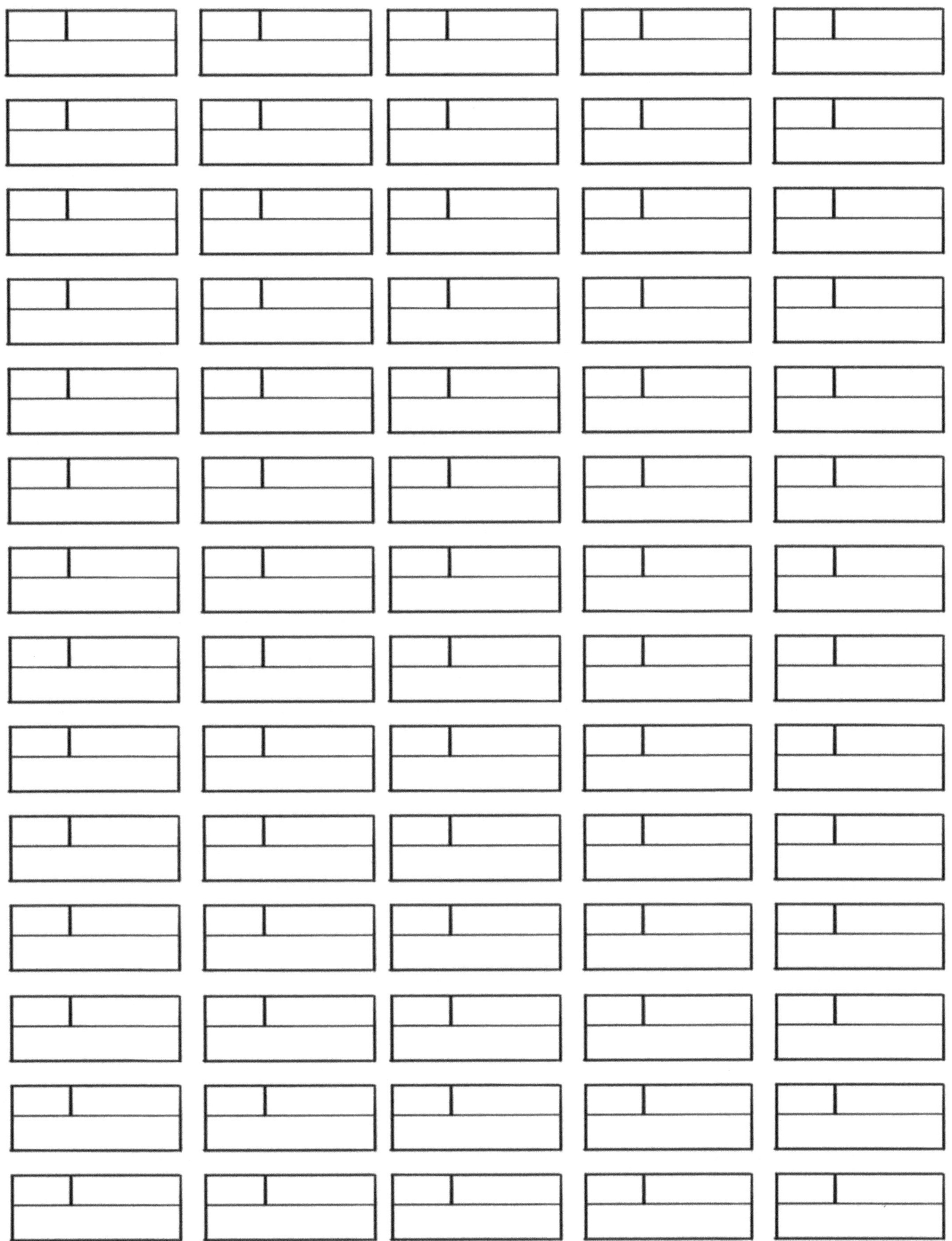

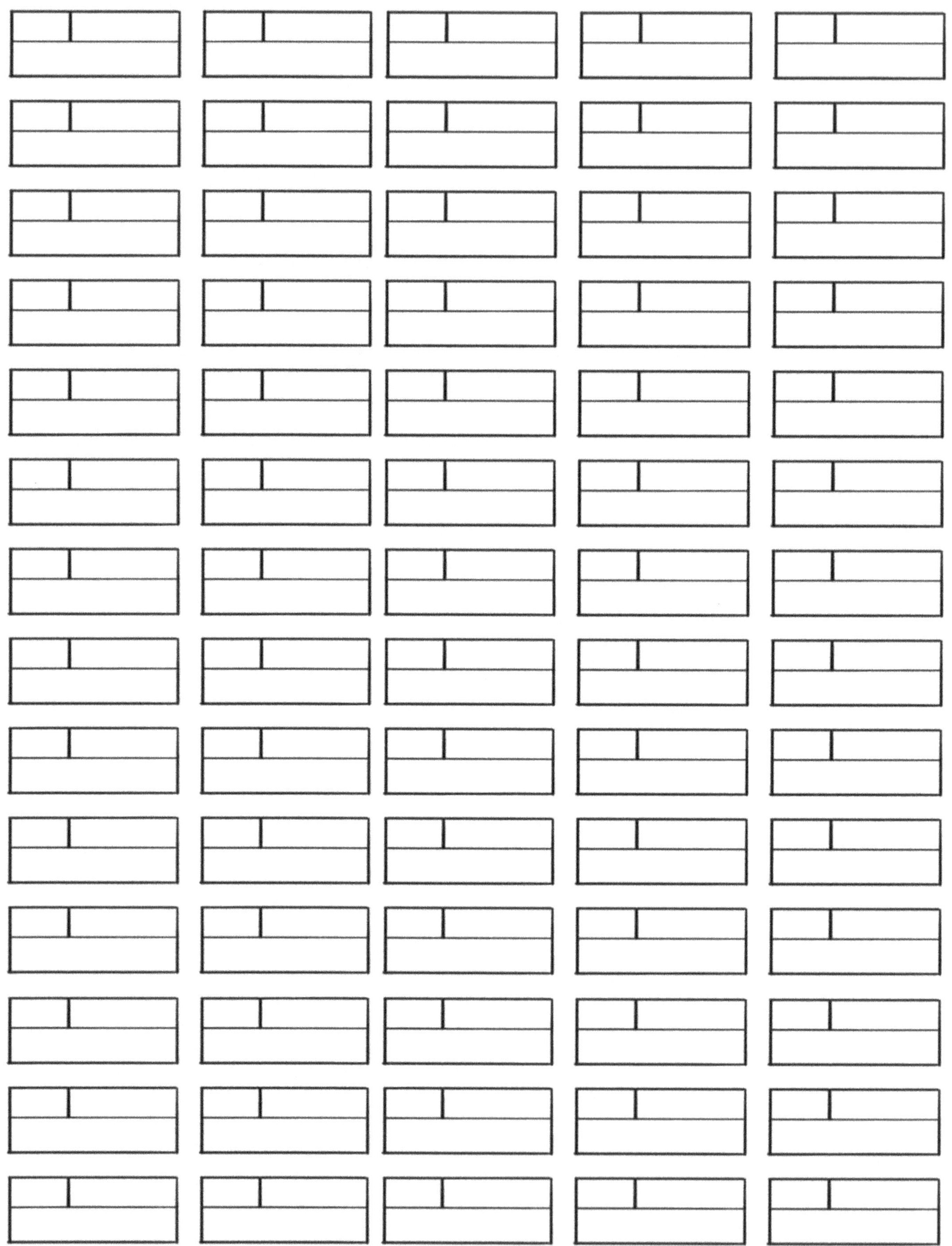

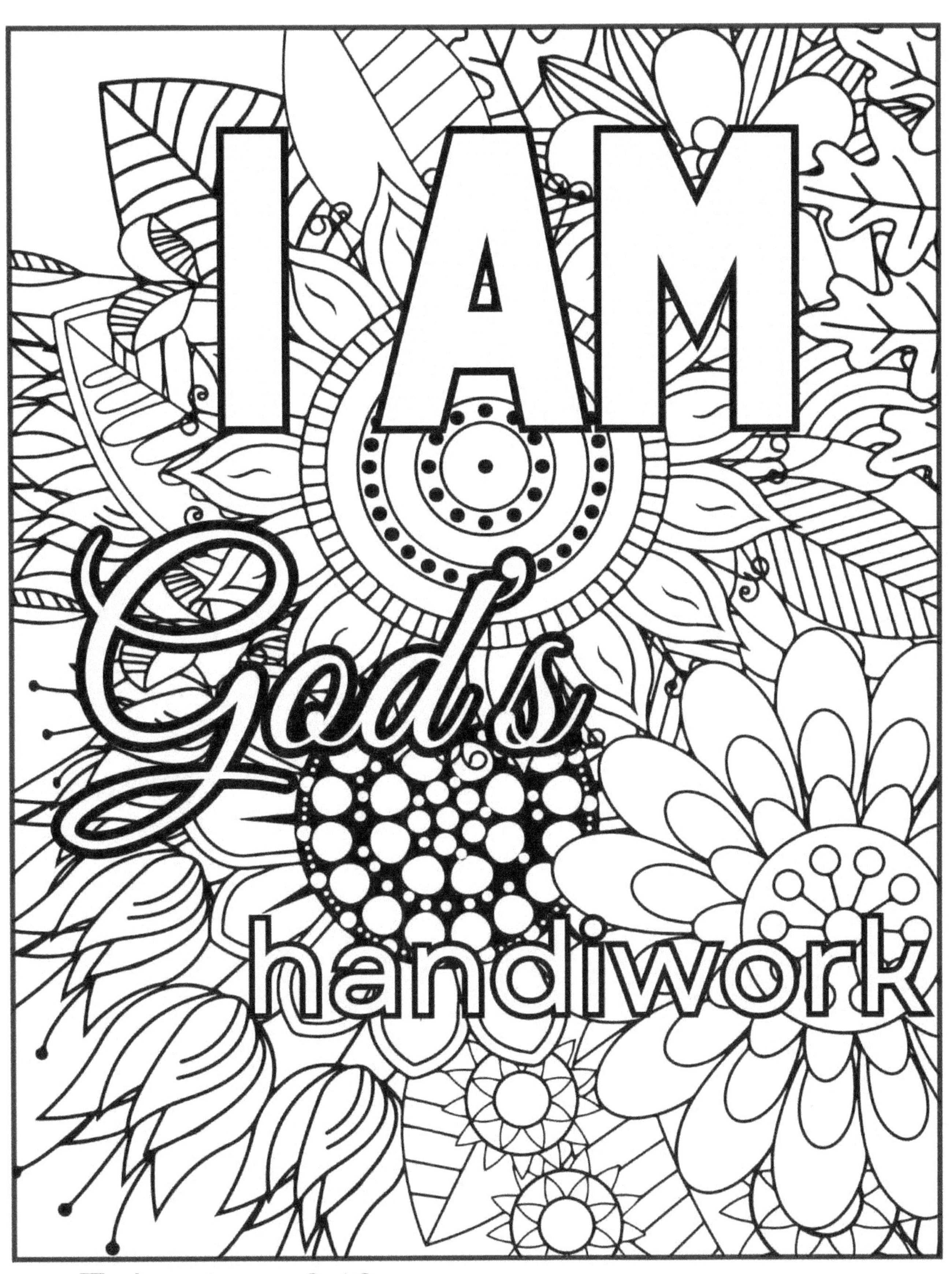

I AM
God's
handiwork
Ephesians 2:10

Scripture in Flowers

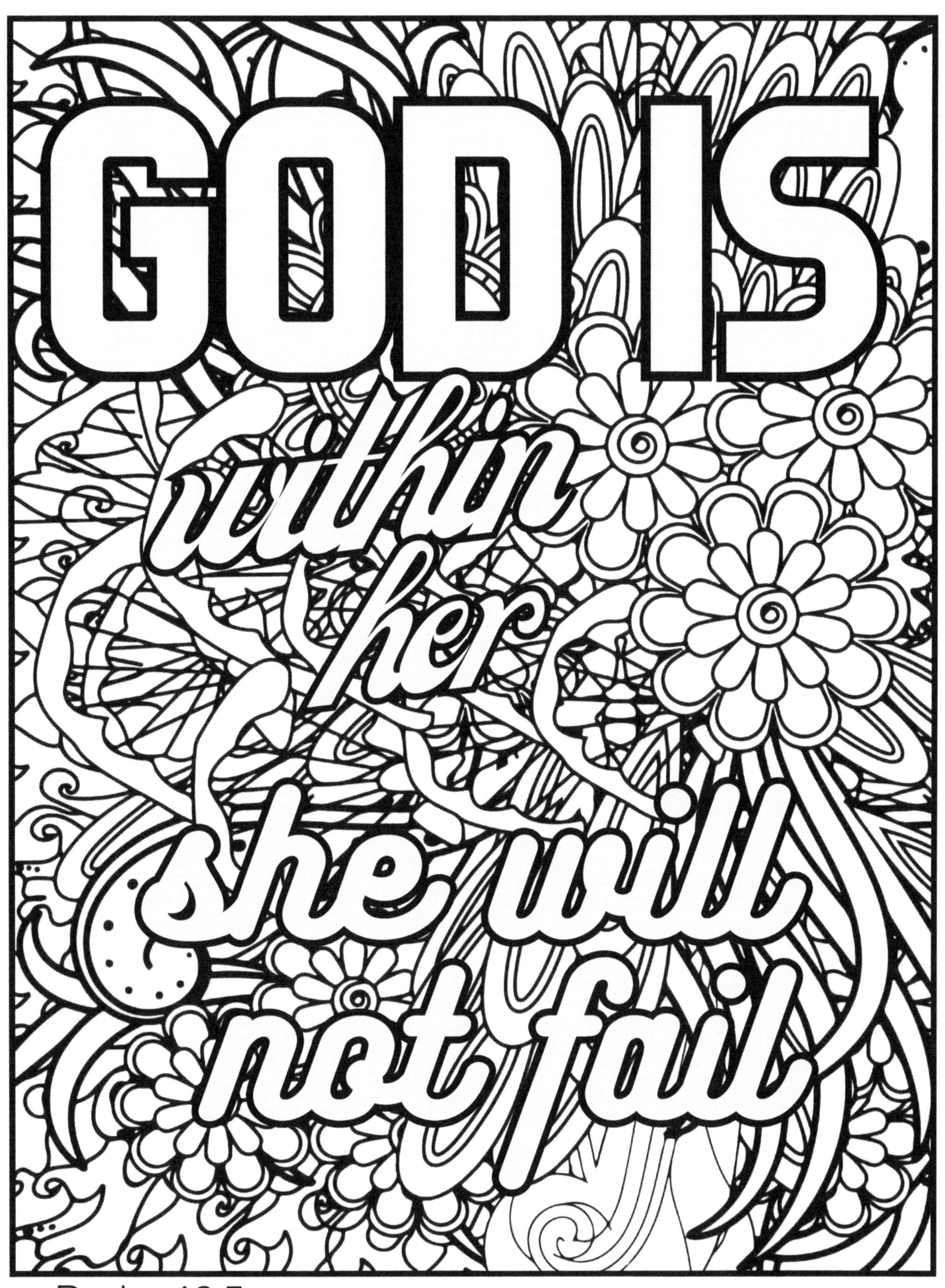

Psalm 46:5

Scripture in Flowers

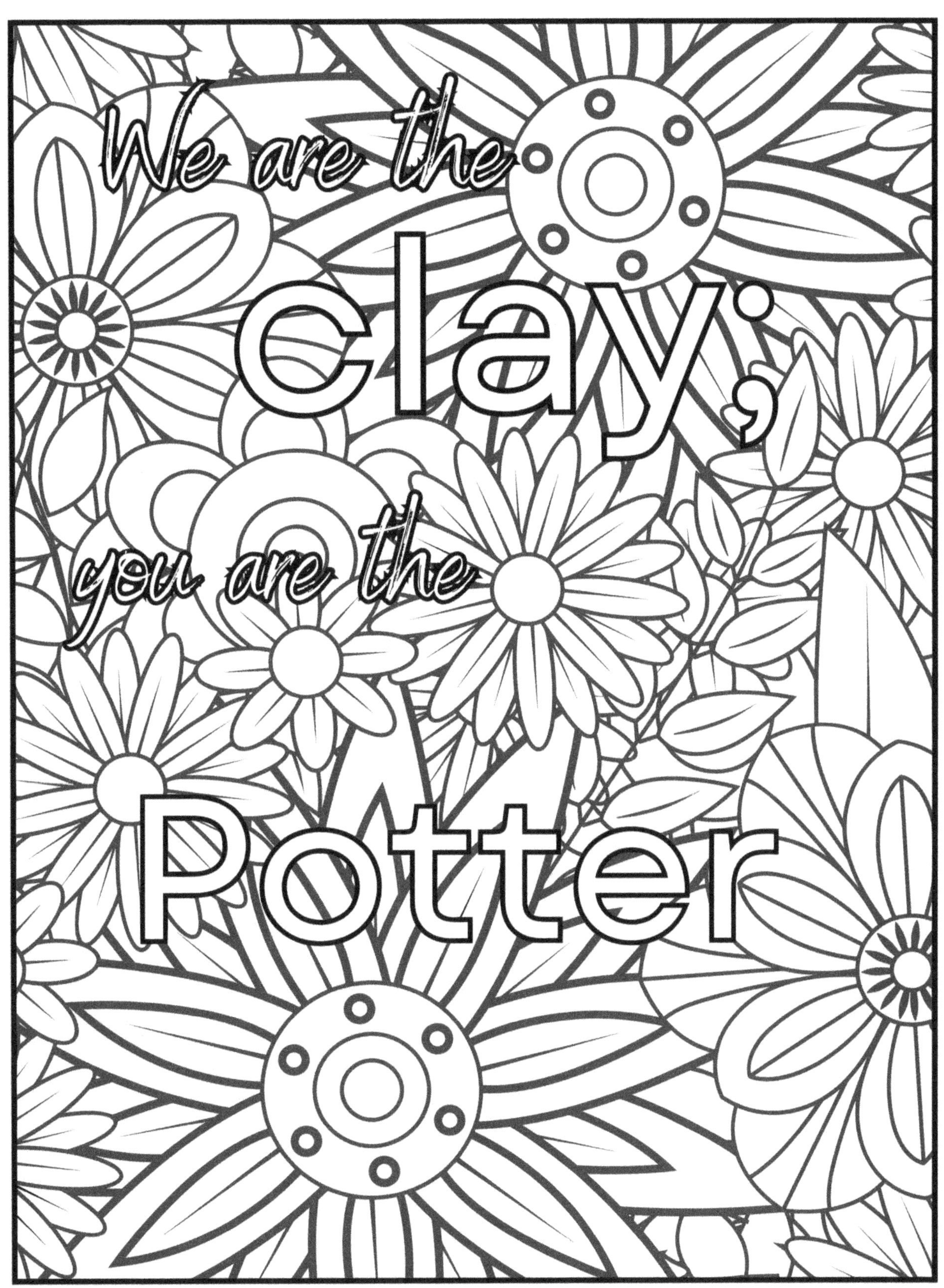

Isaiah 64:8

Scripture in
Flowers

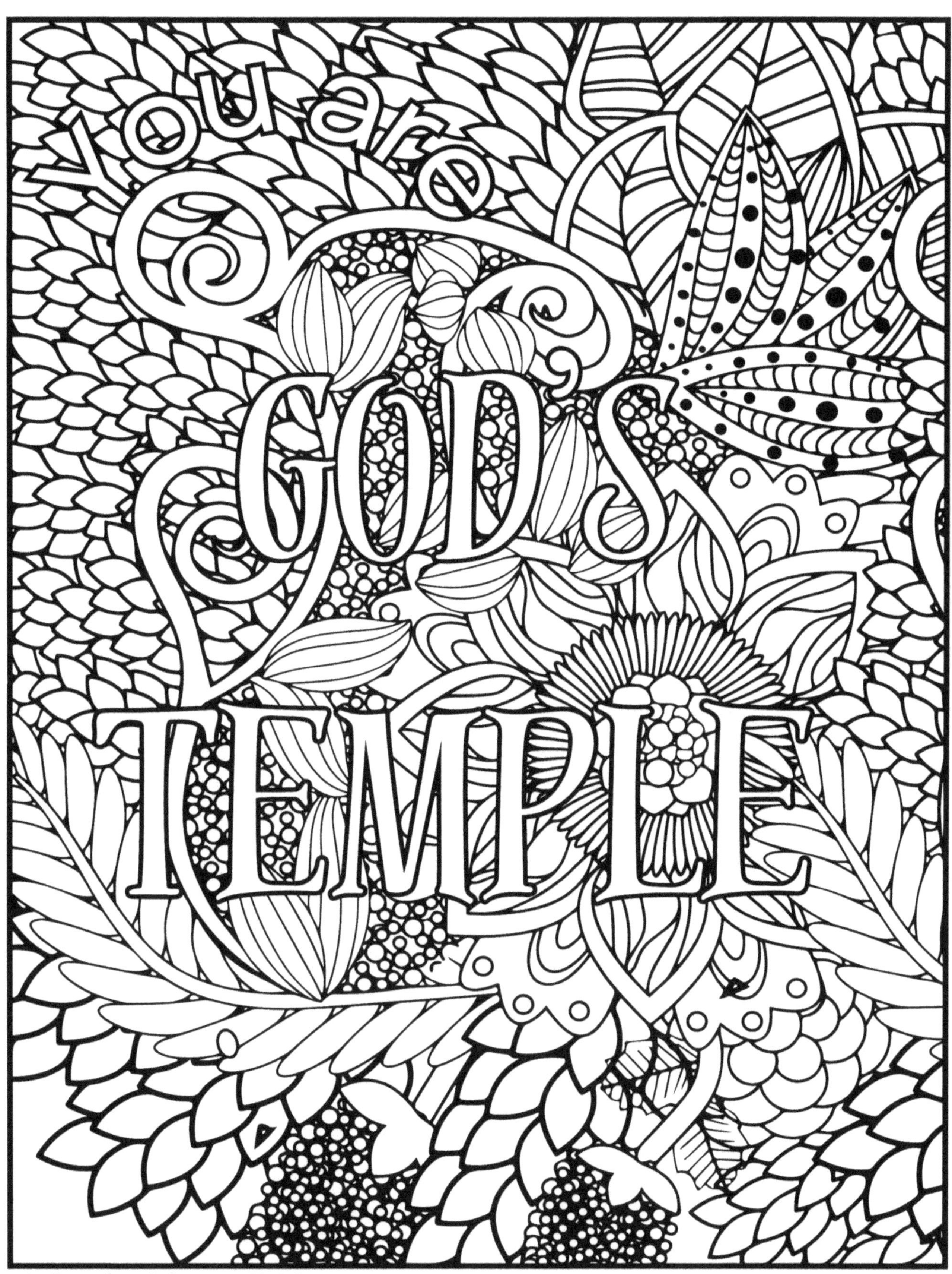

1 Corinthians 3:16

Scripture in Flowers

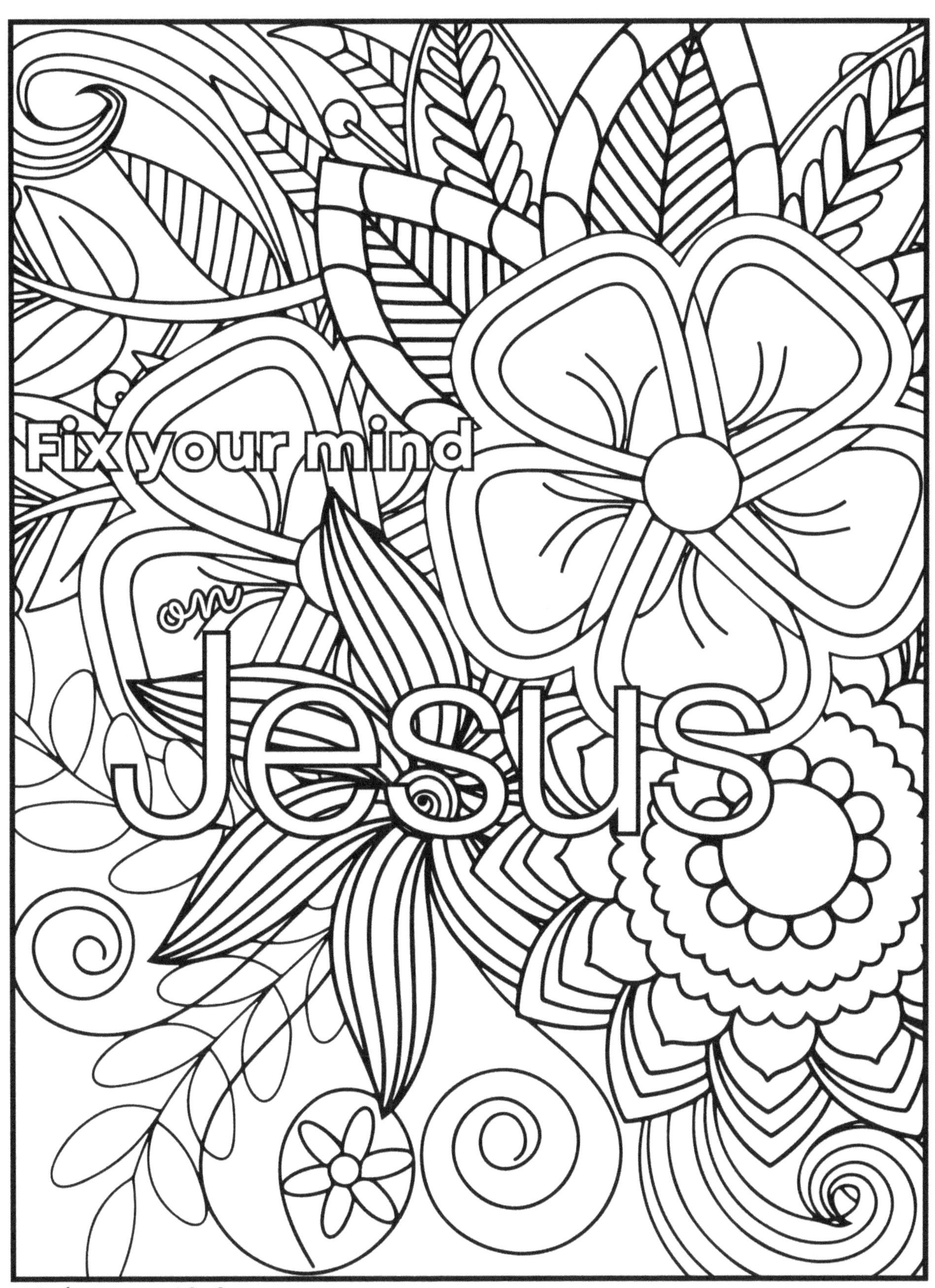

Hebrews 12:2

Scripture in Flowers

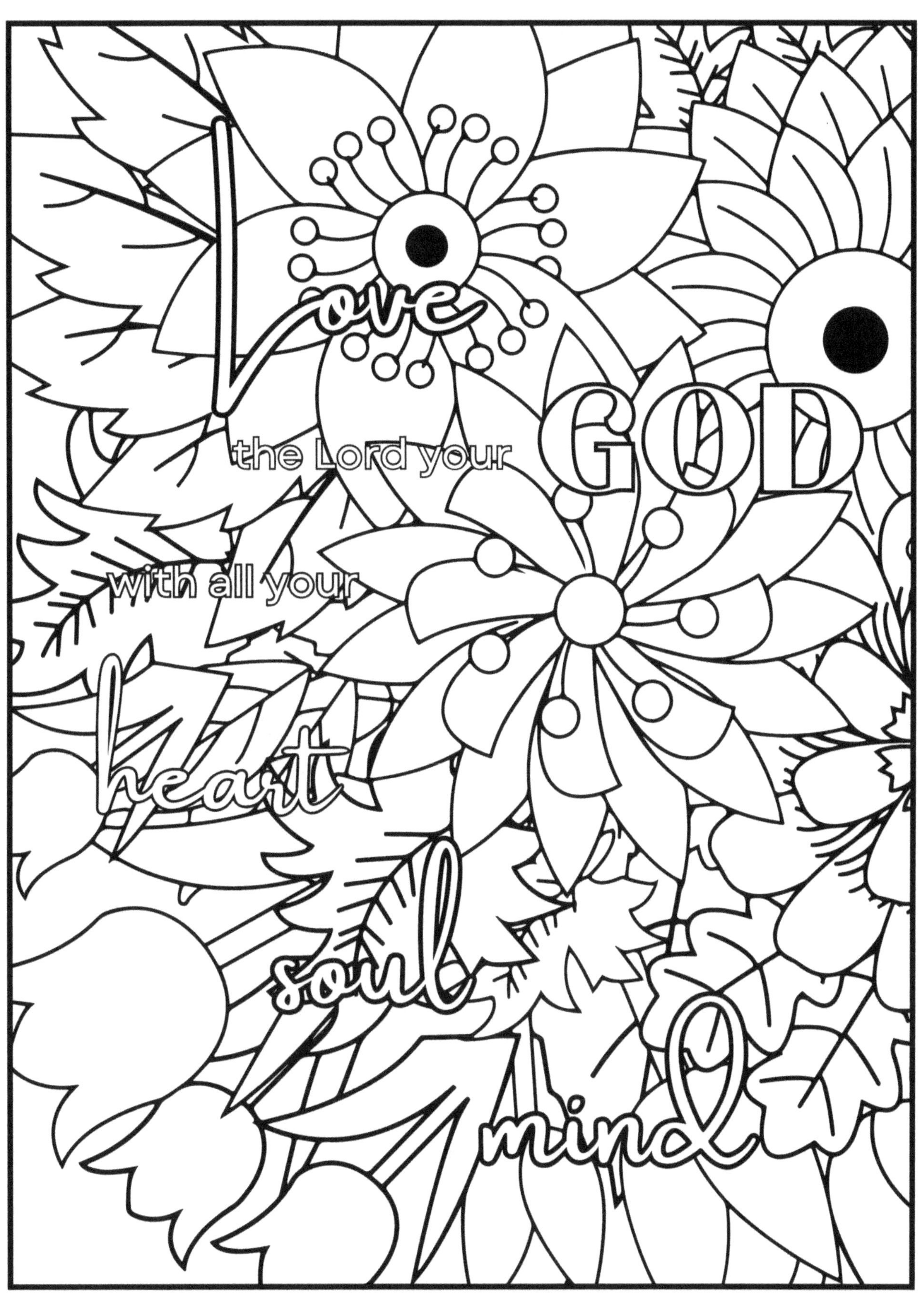

Love
the Lord your GOD
with all your
heart
soul
mind

Scripture in
Flowers

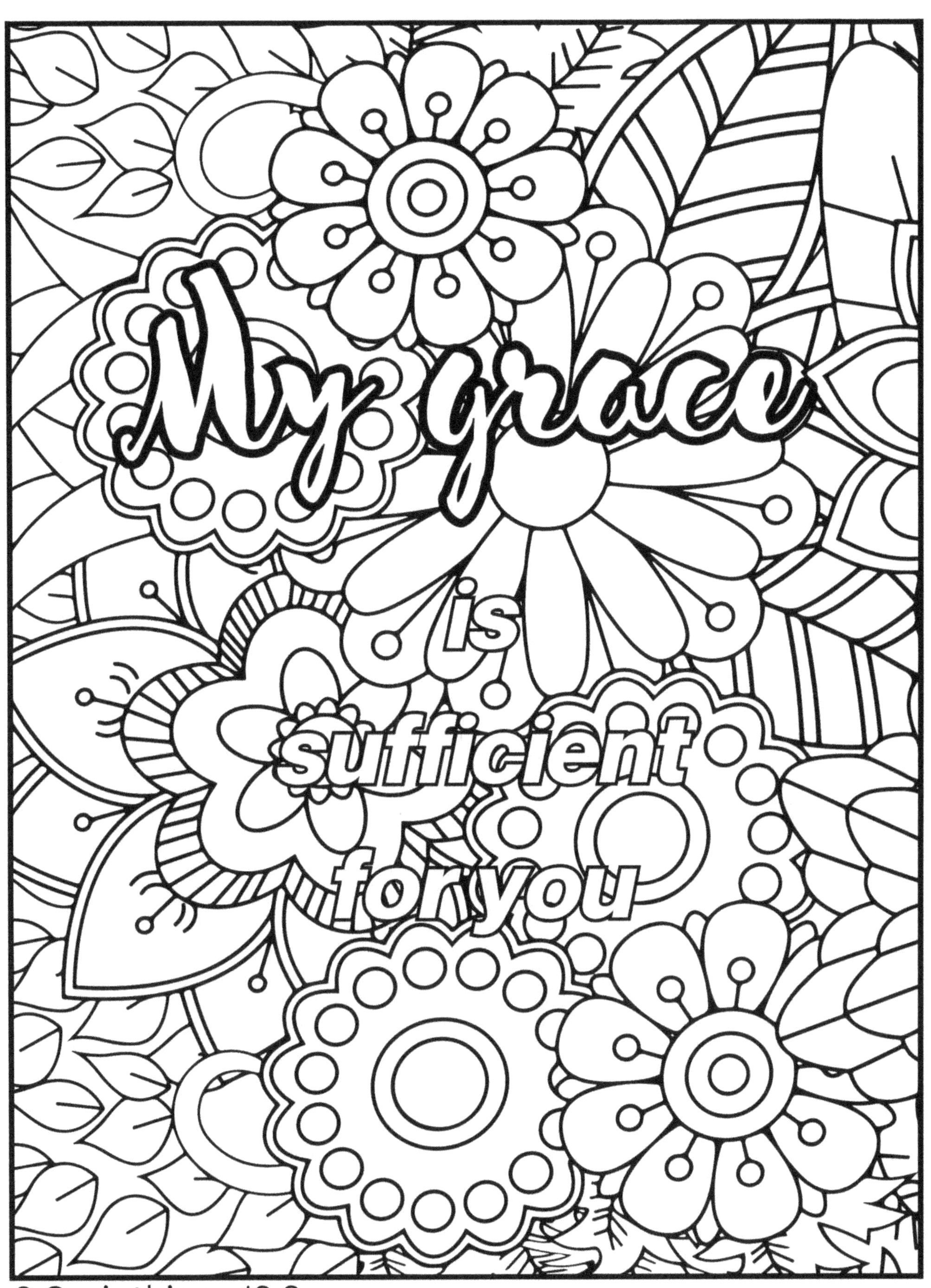

2 Corinthians 12:9

Scripture in Flowers

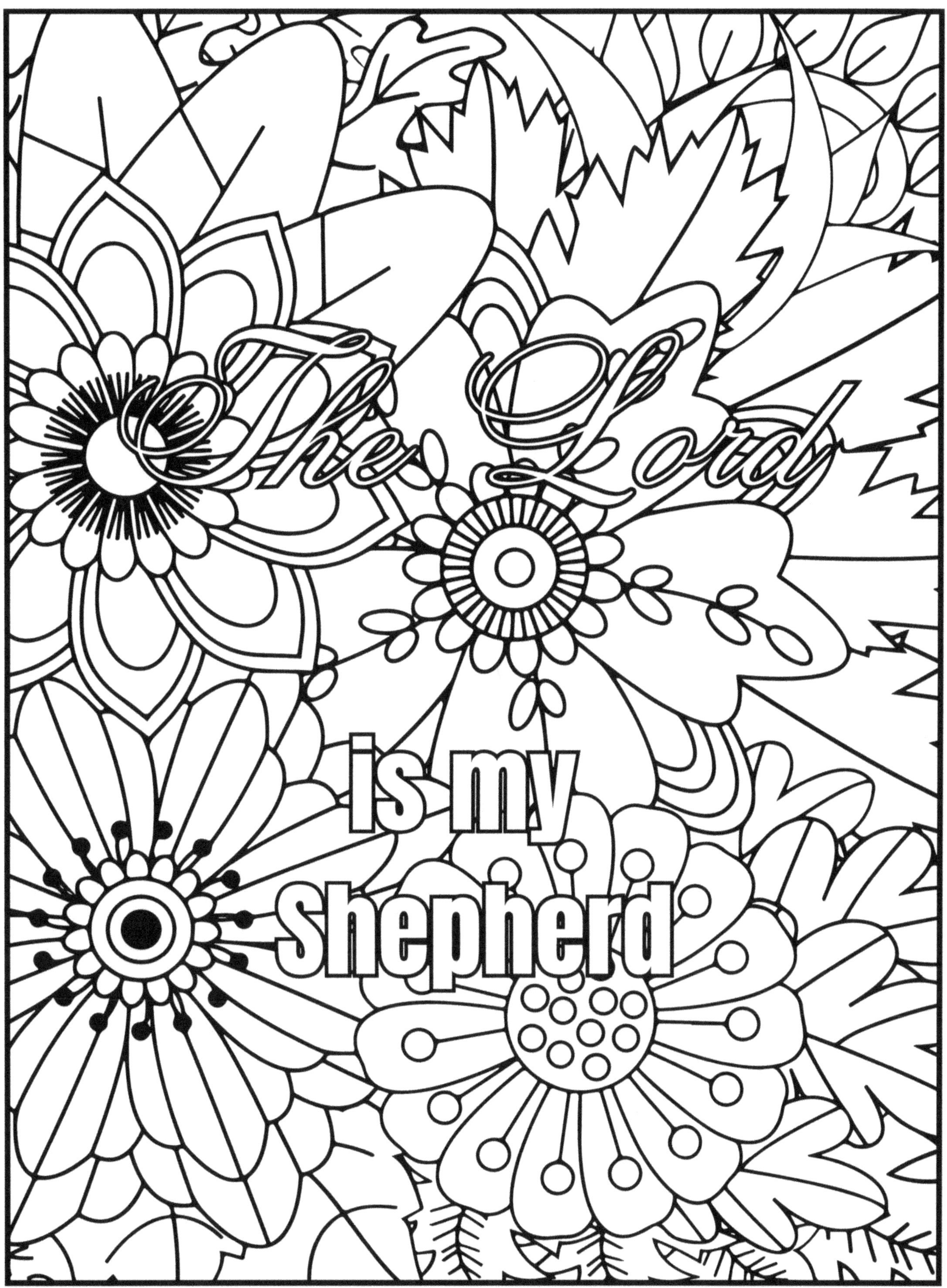

Psalm 23:1

Scripture in Flowers

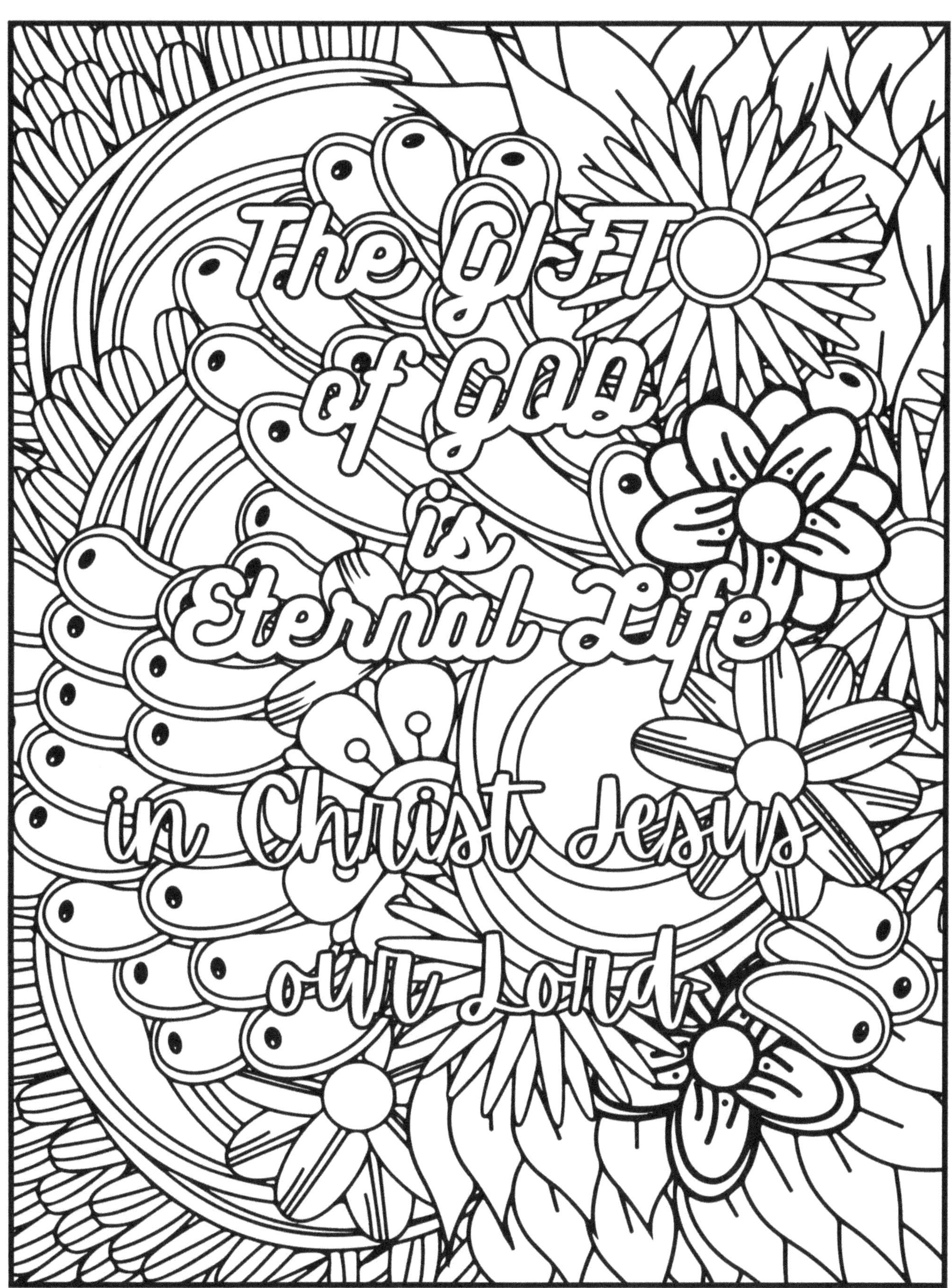

Romans 6:23

Scripture in Flowers

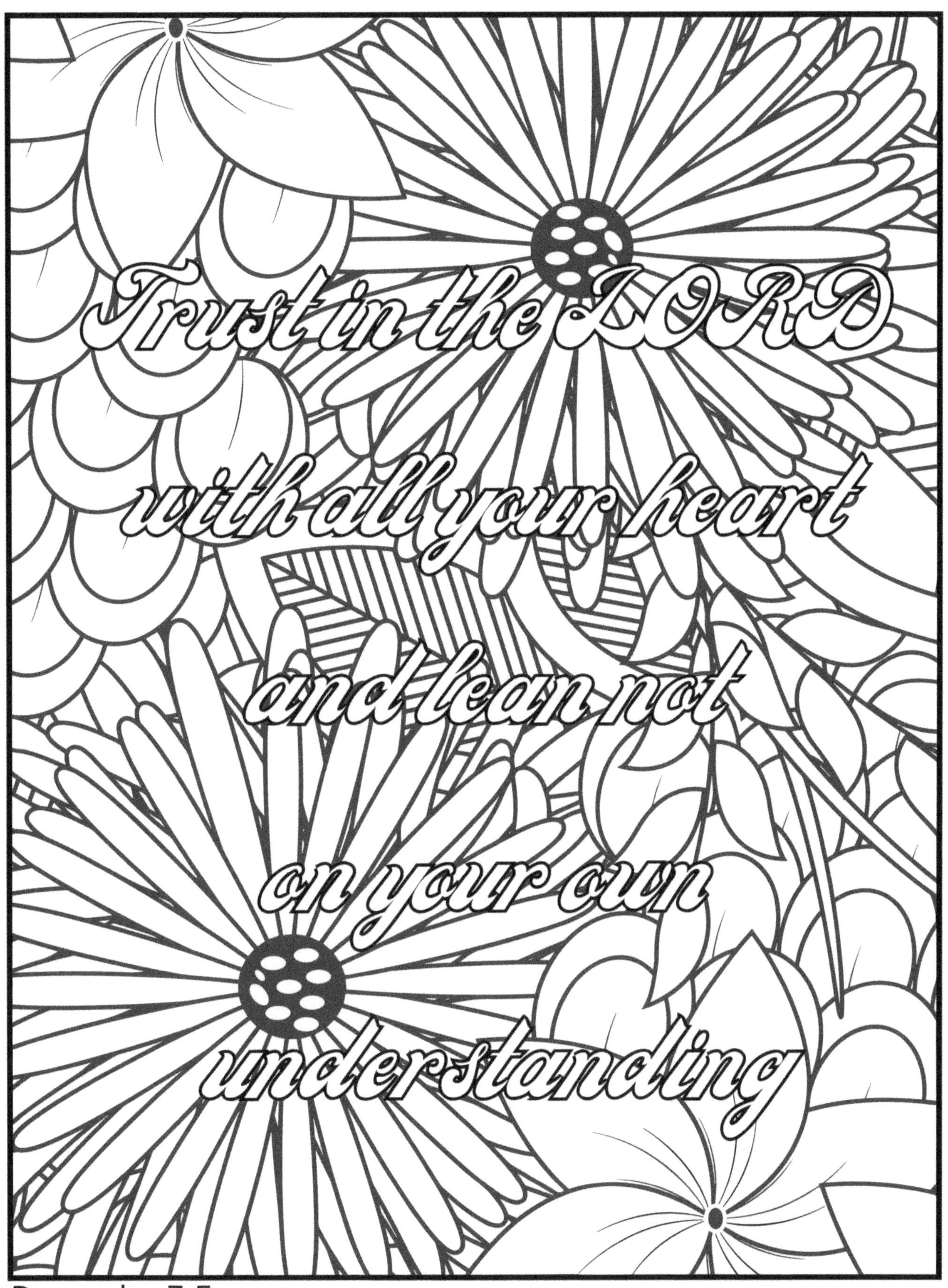

Trust in the LORD
with all your heart
and lean not
on your own
understanding

Proverbs 3:5

Scripture in Flowers

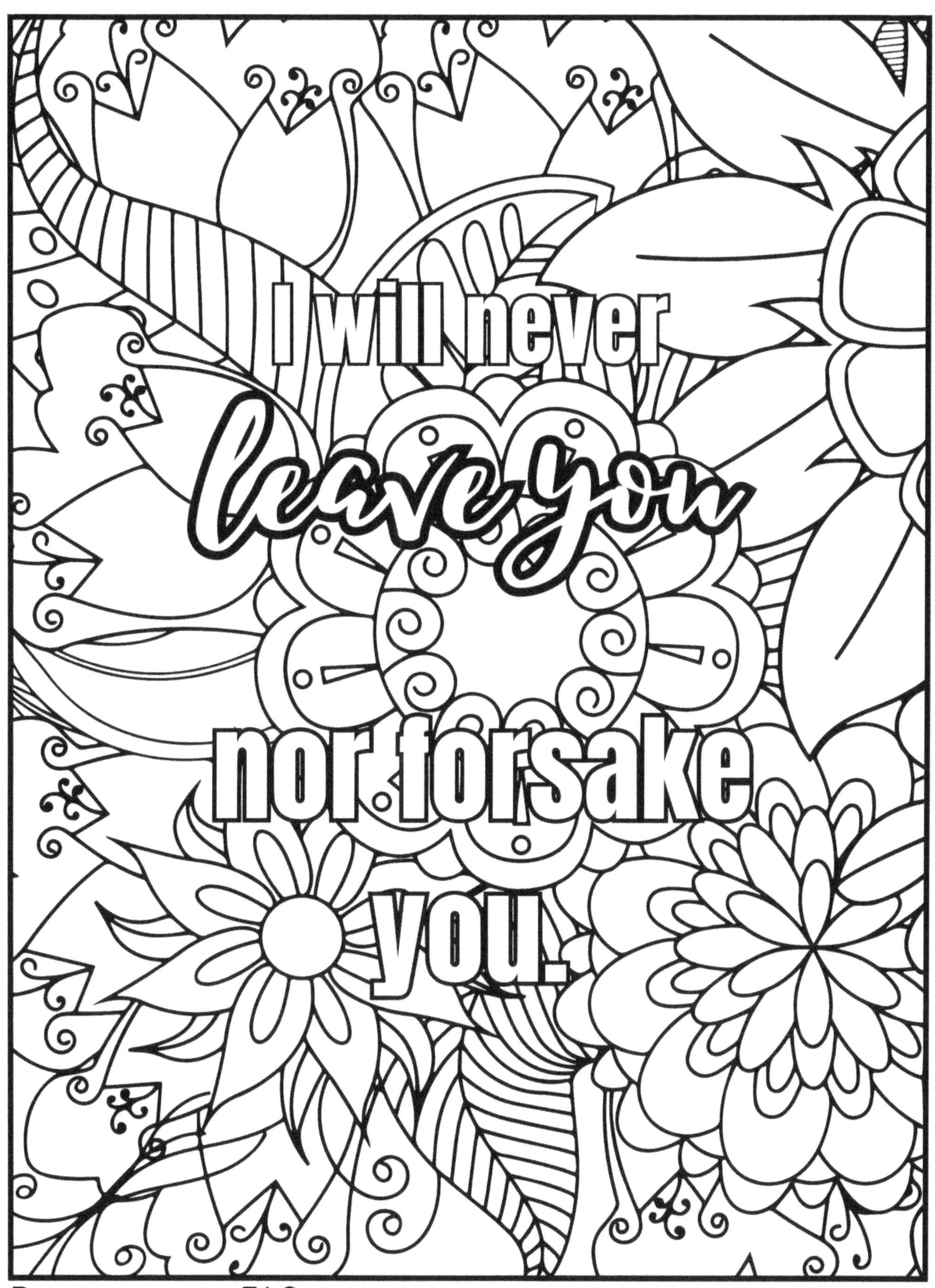

Deuteronomy 31:8

Scripture in Flowers

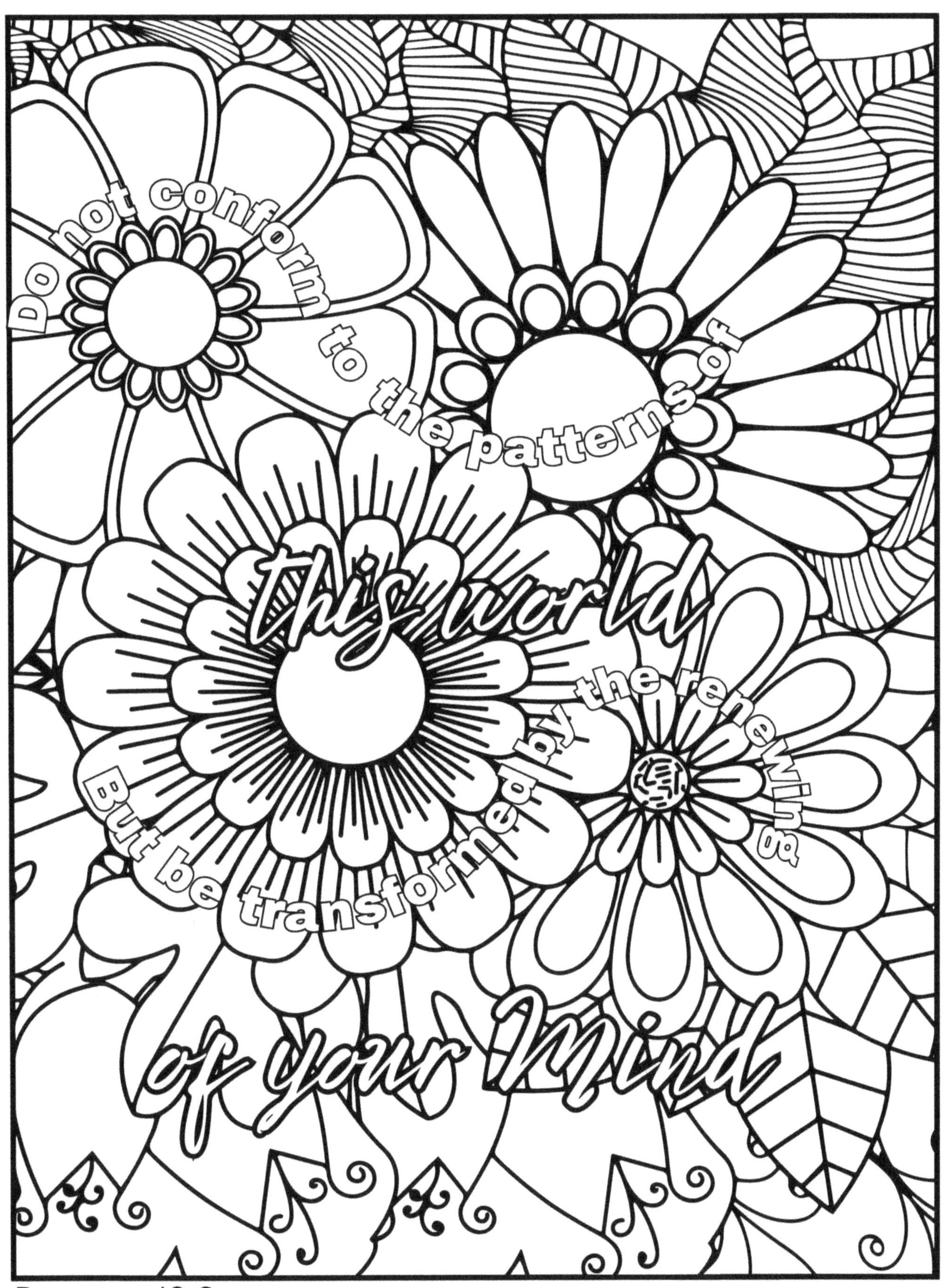

Do not conform to the patterns of
this world
But be transformed by the renewing
of your Mind

Romans 12:2

Scripture in
Flowers

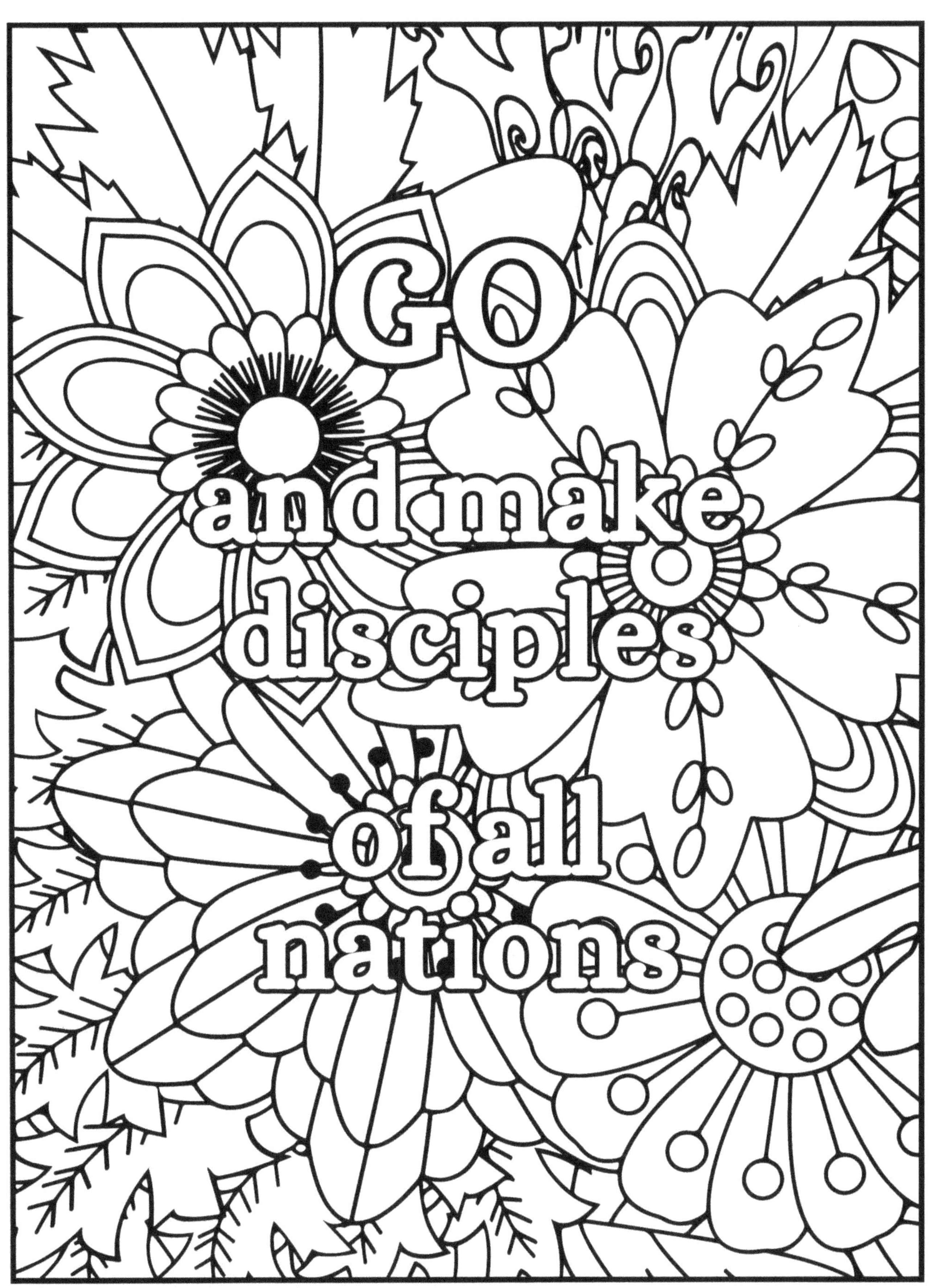

Matthew 28:19

Scripture in Flowers

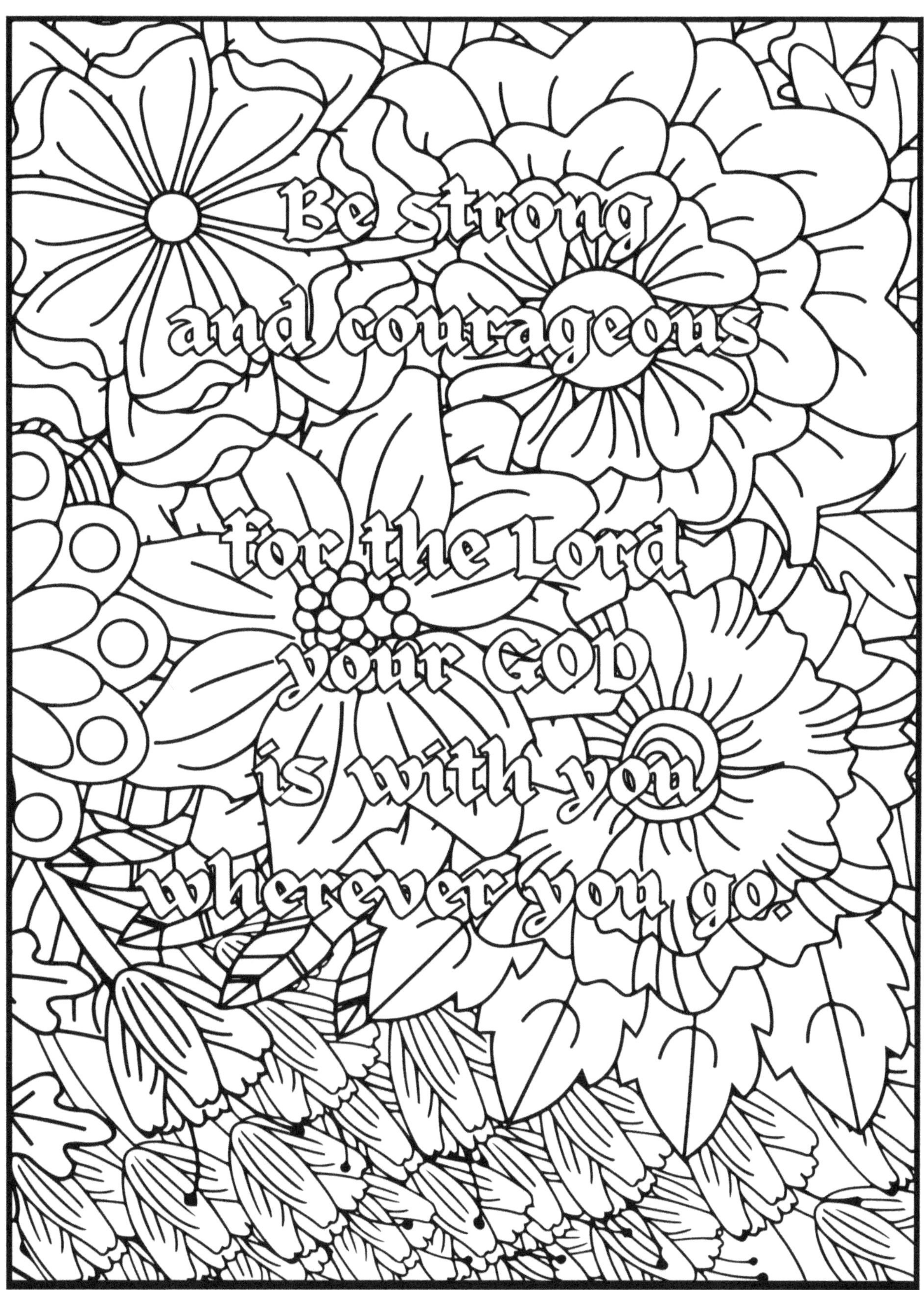

Be strong
and courageous
for the Lord
your God
is with you
wherever you go.

Joshua 1:9

Scripture in Flowers

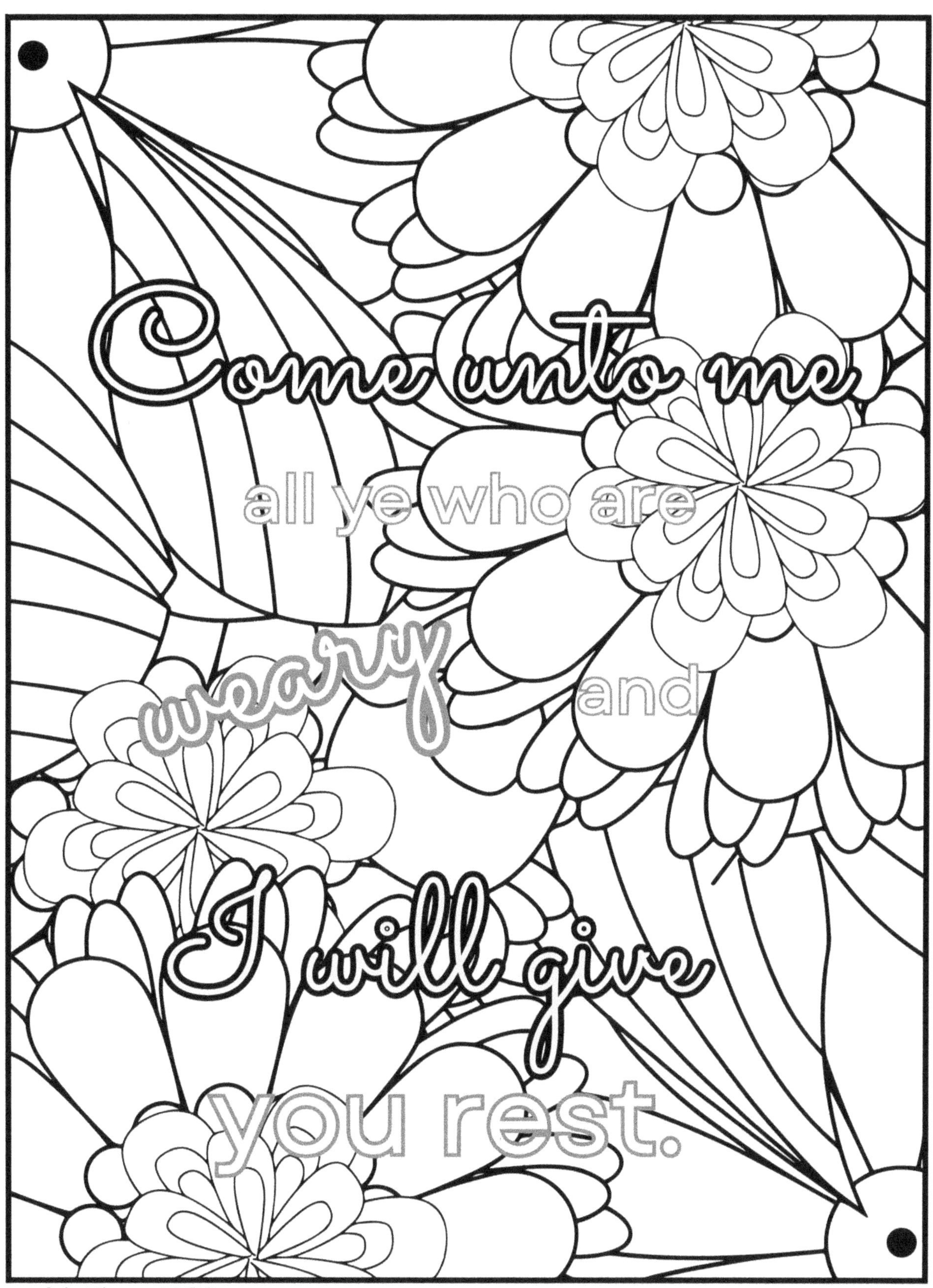

Come unto me
all ye who are
weary and
I will give
you rest.
Matthew 11:28

Scripture in
Flowers

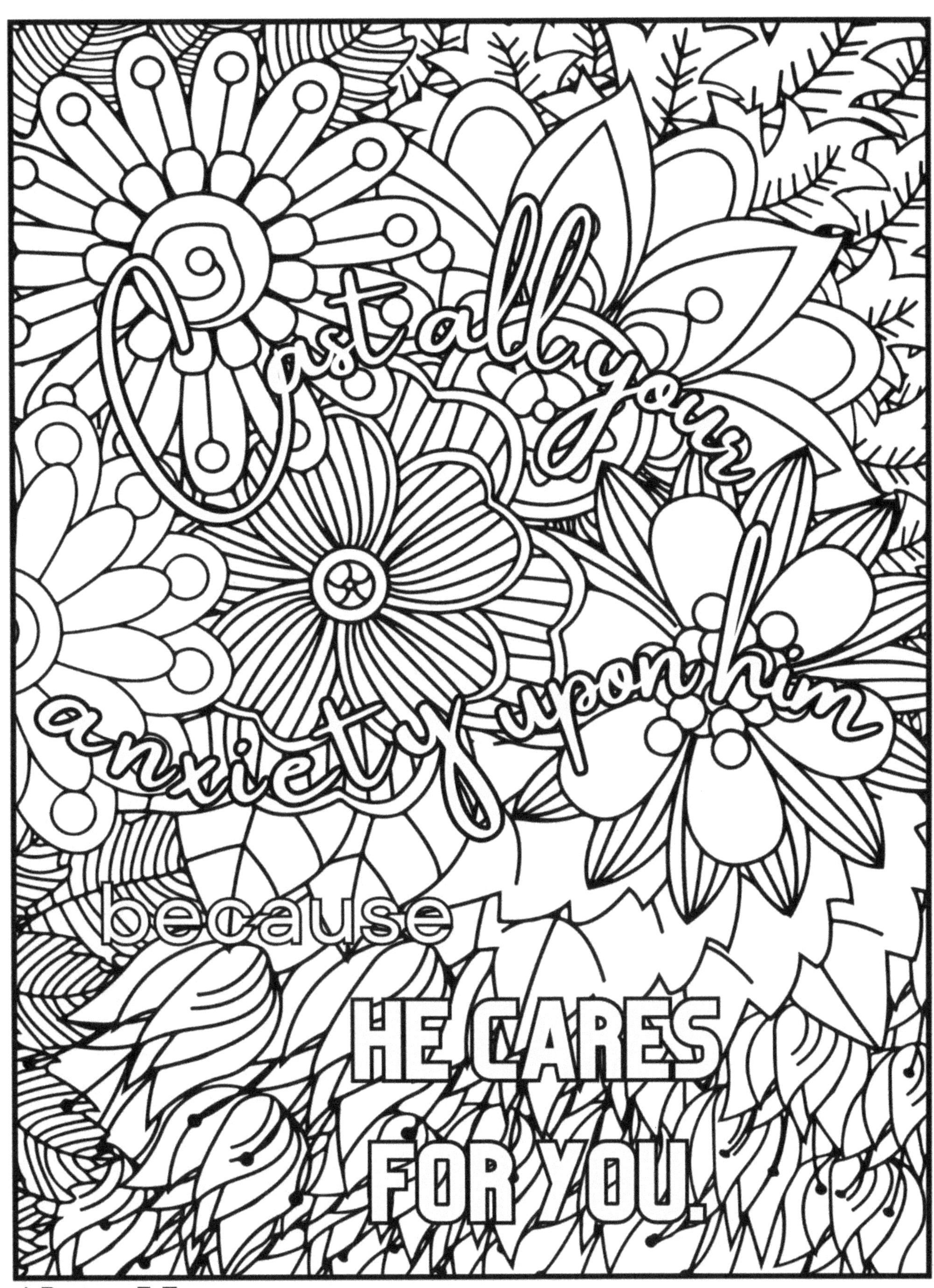

1 Peter 5:7

Scripture in Flowers

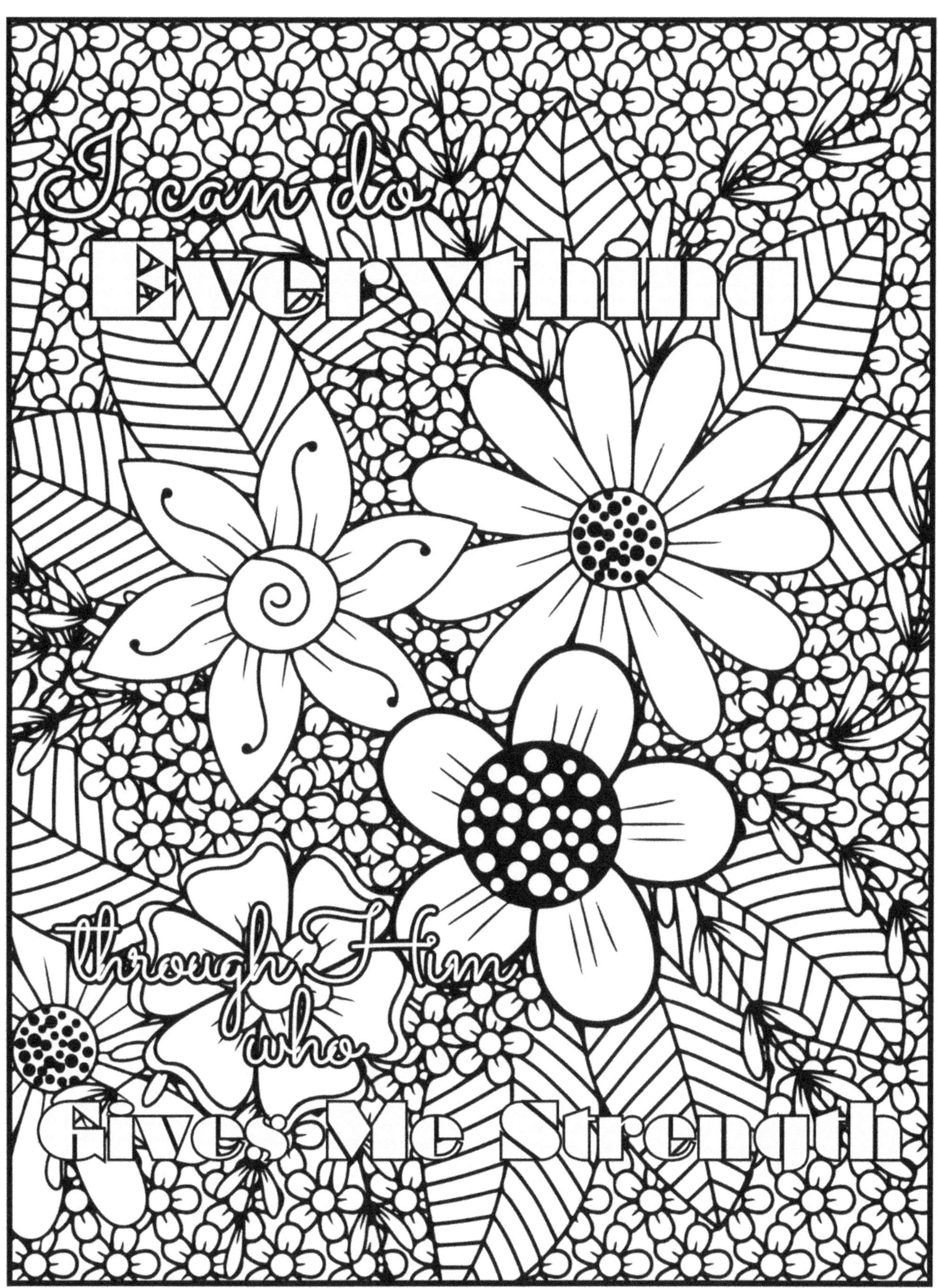

Philippians 4:13

Scripture in Flowers

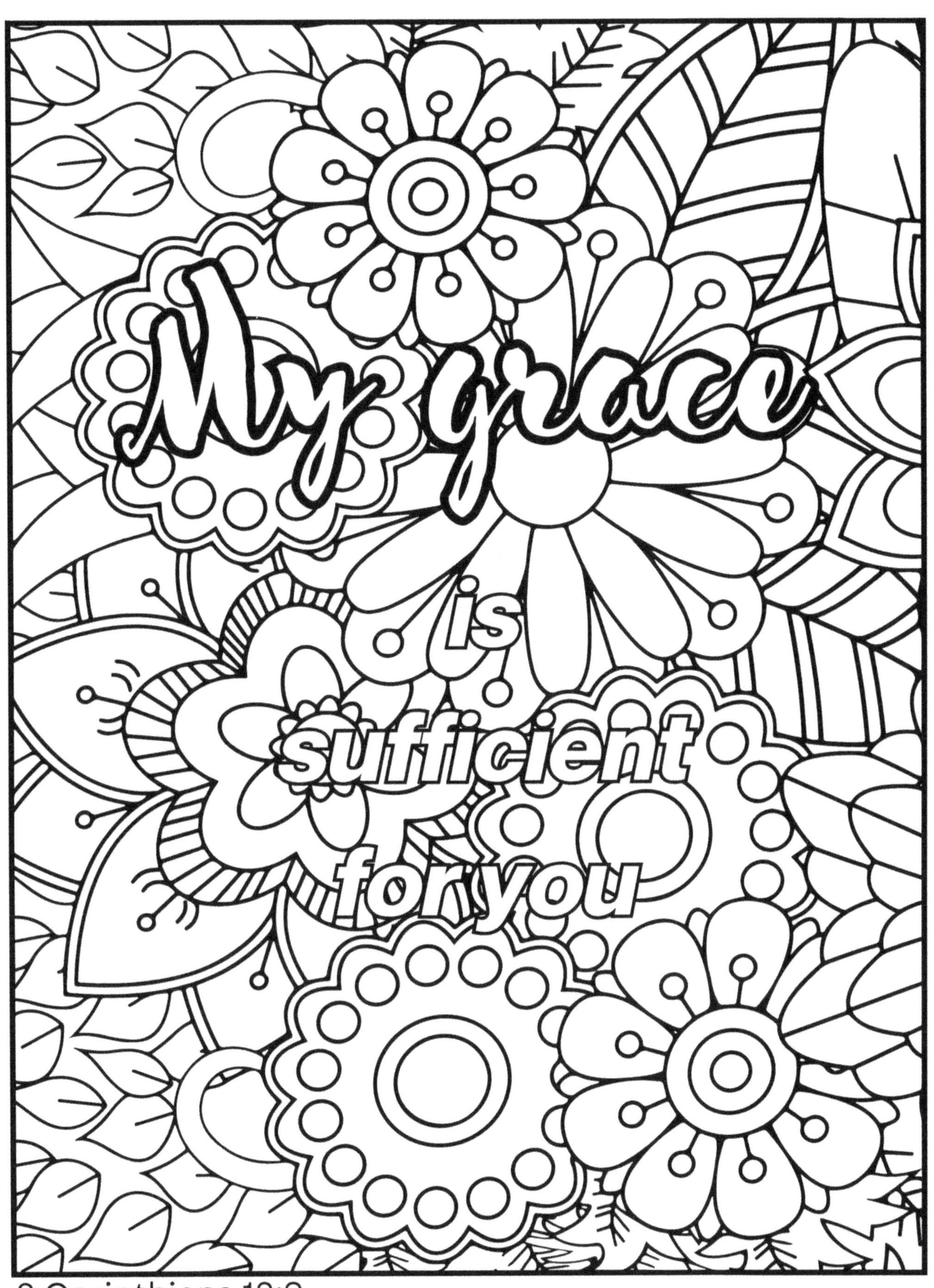

2 Corinthians 12:9

Scripture in Flowers

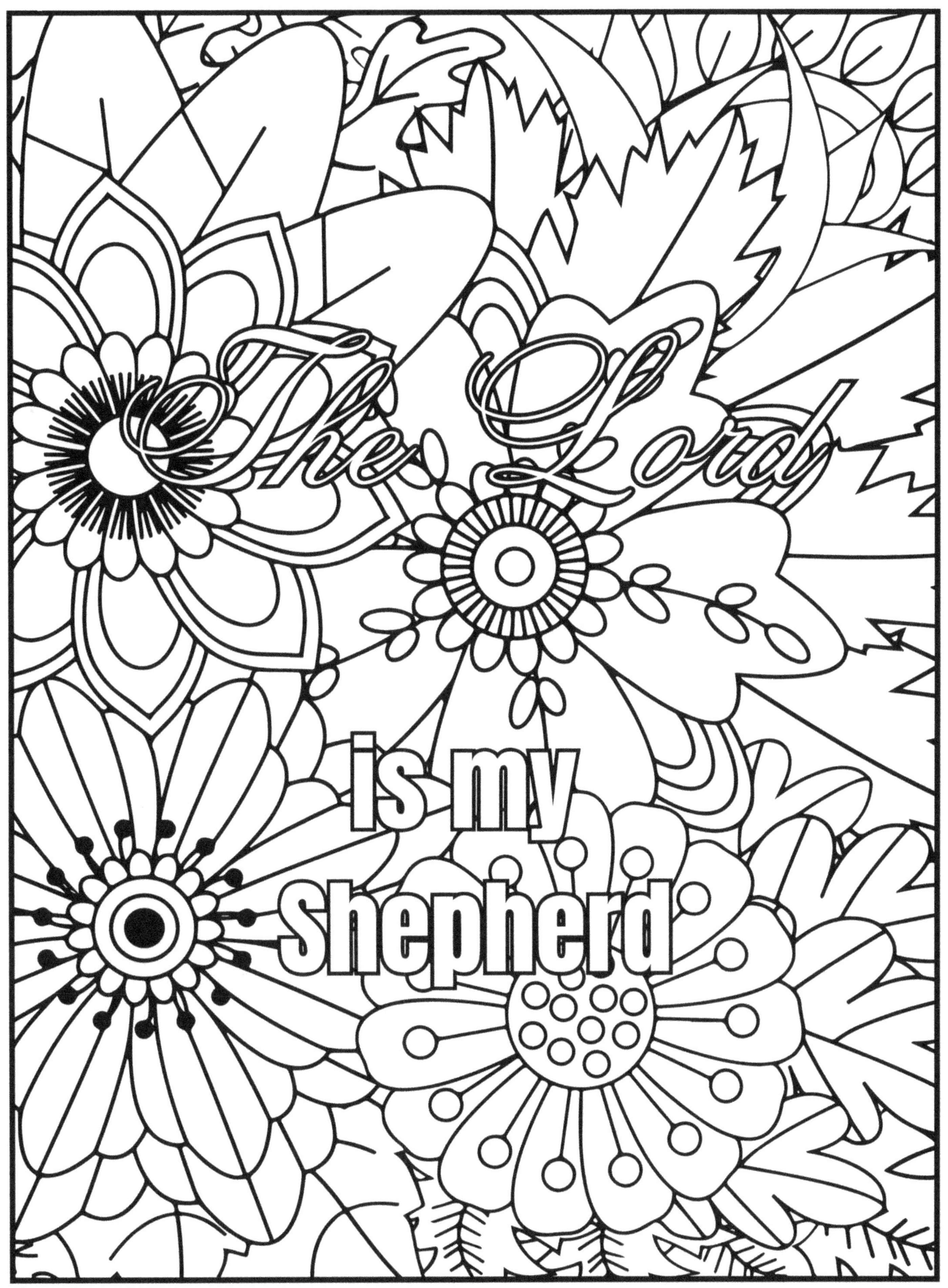

Psalm 23:1

Scripture in
Flowers

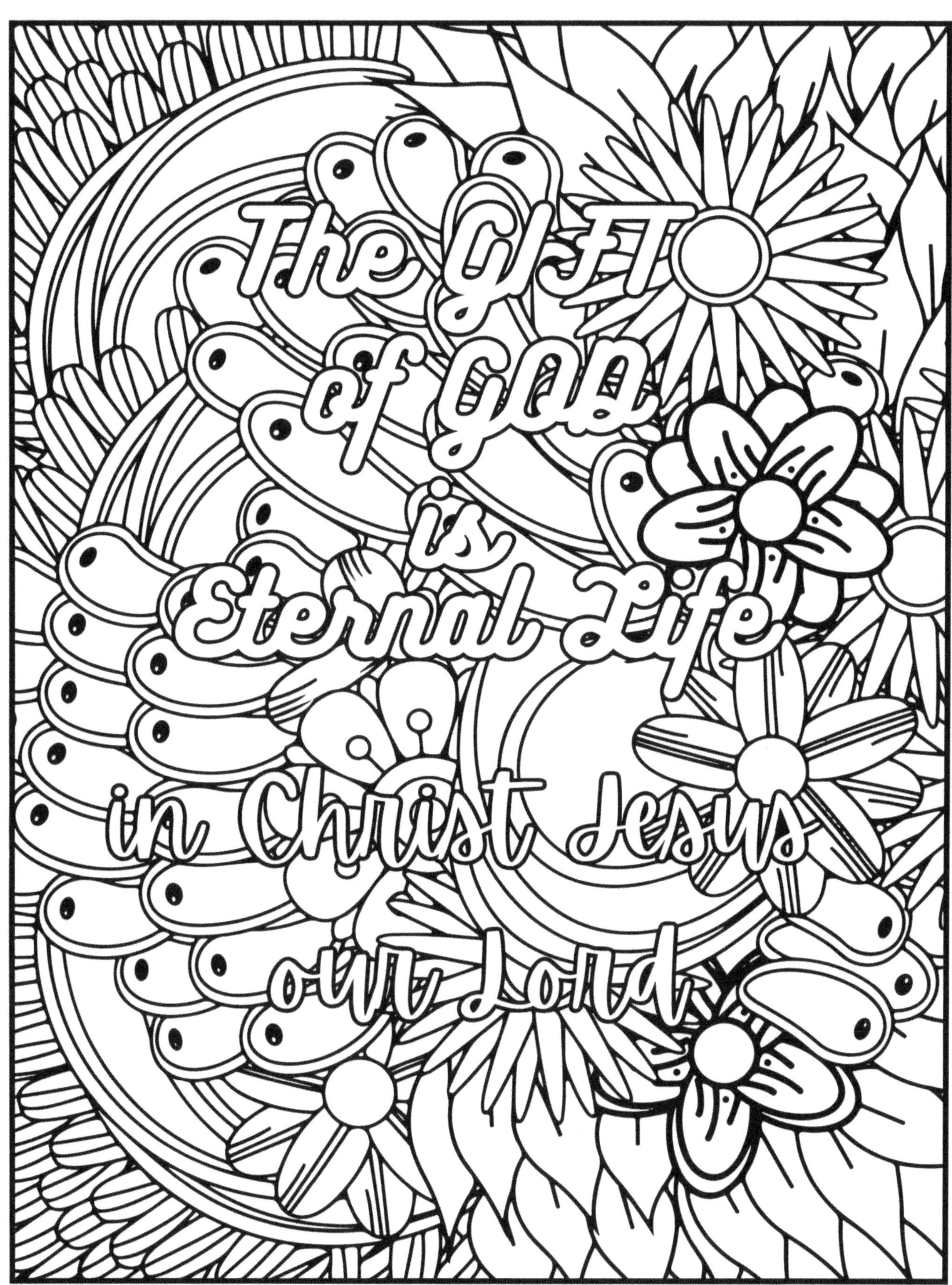

Romans 6:23

Scripture in Flowers

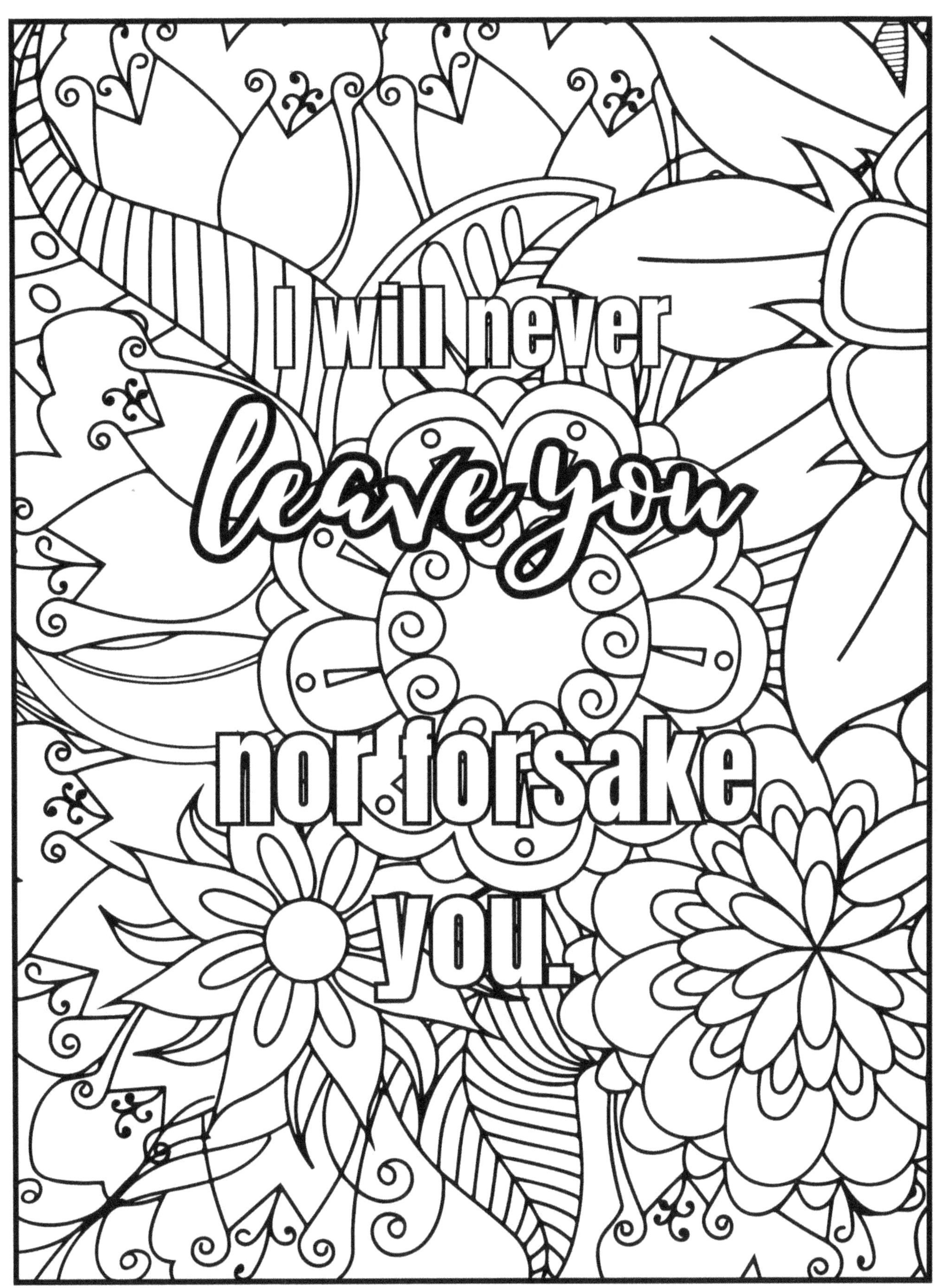

Deuteronomy 31:8

Scripture in
Flowers

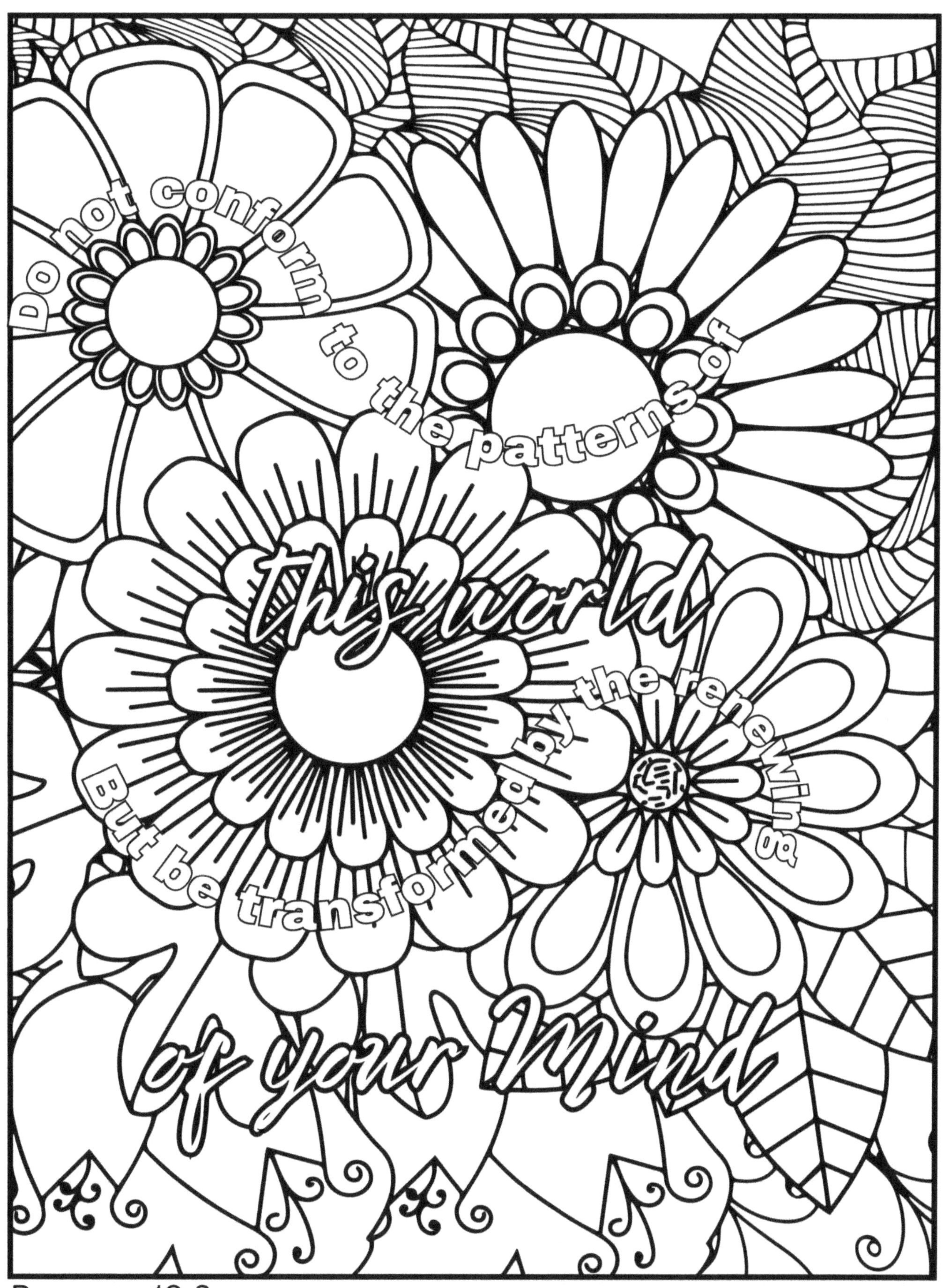

Do not conform to the pattern of this world
But be transformed by the renewing of your Mind
Romans 12:2

Scripture in
Flowers

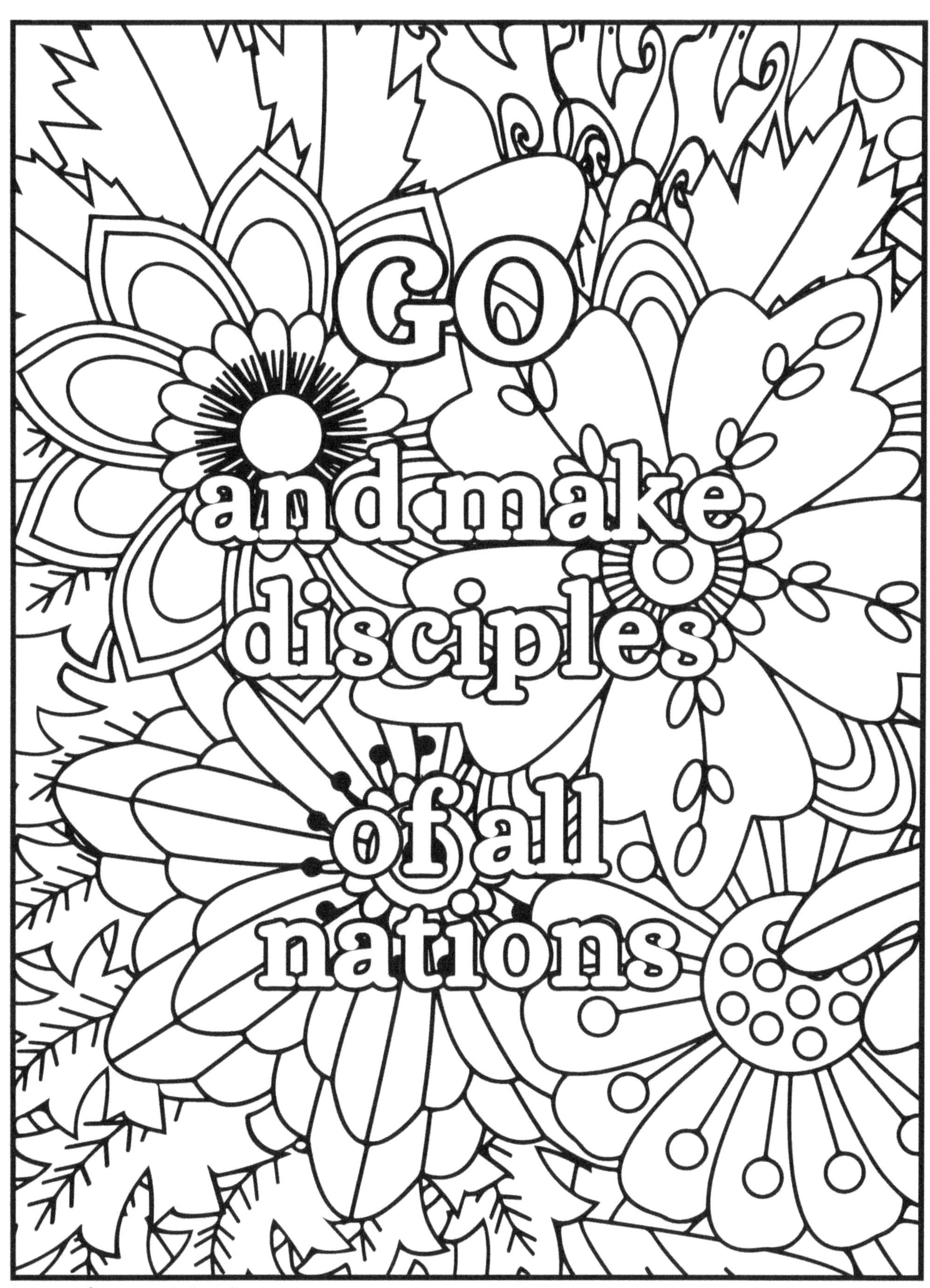

Matthew 28:19

Scripture in Flowers

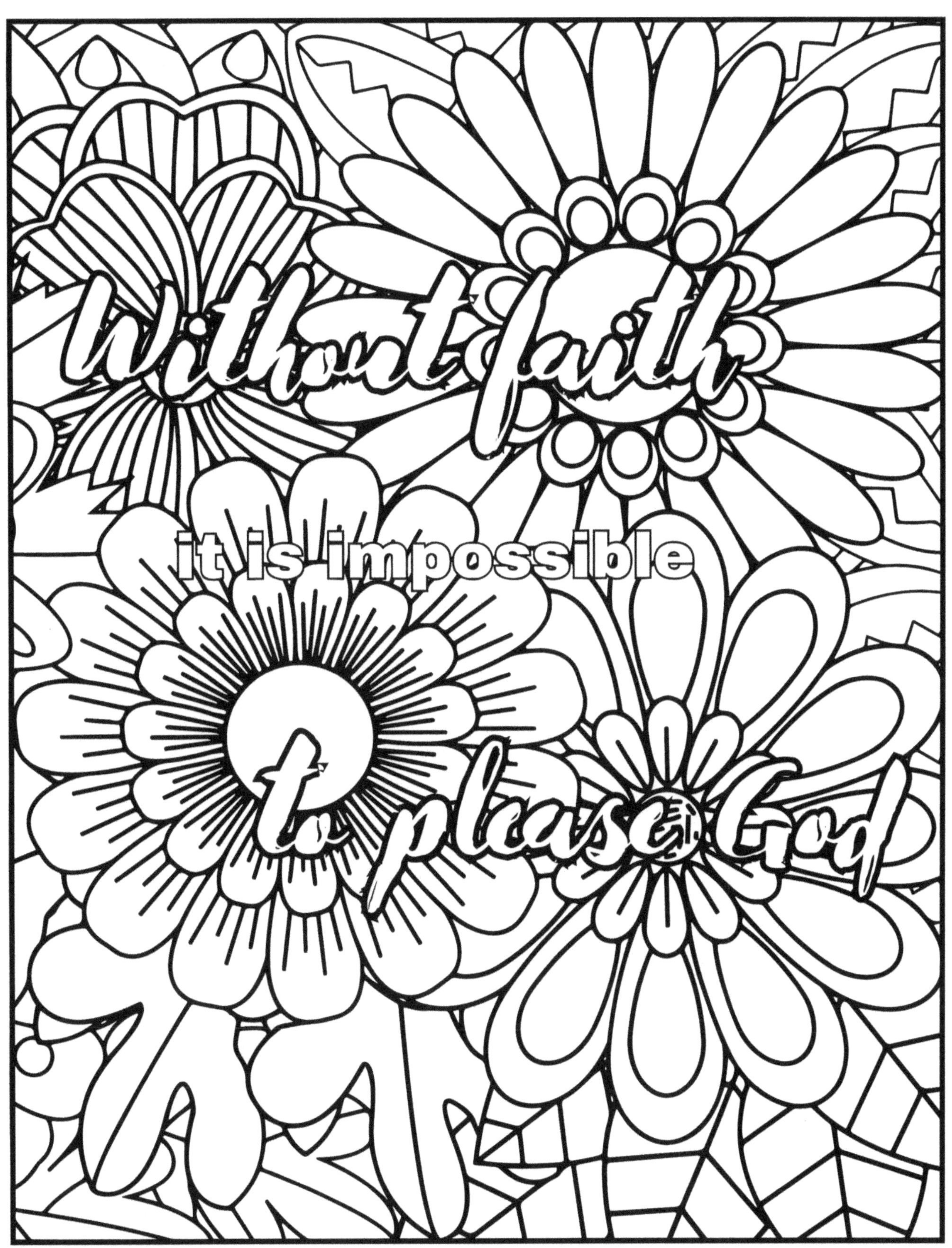

Hebrews 11:6

Scripture in
Flowers

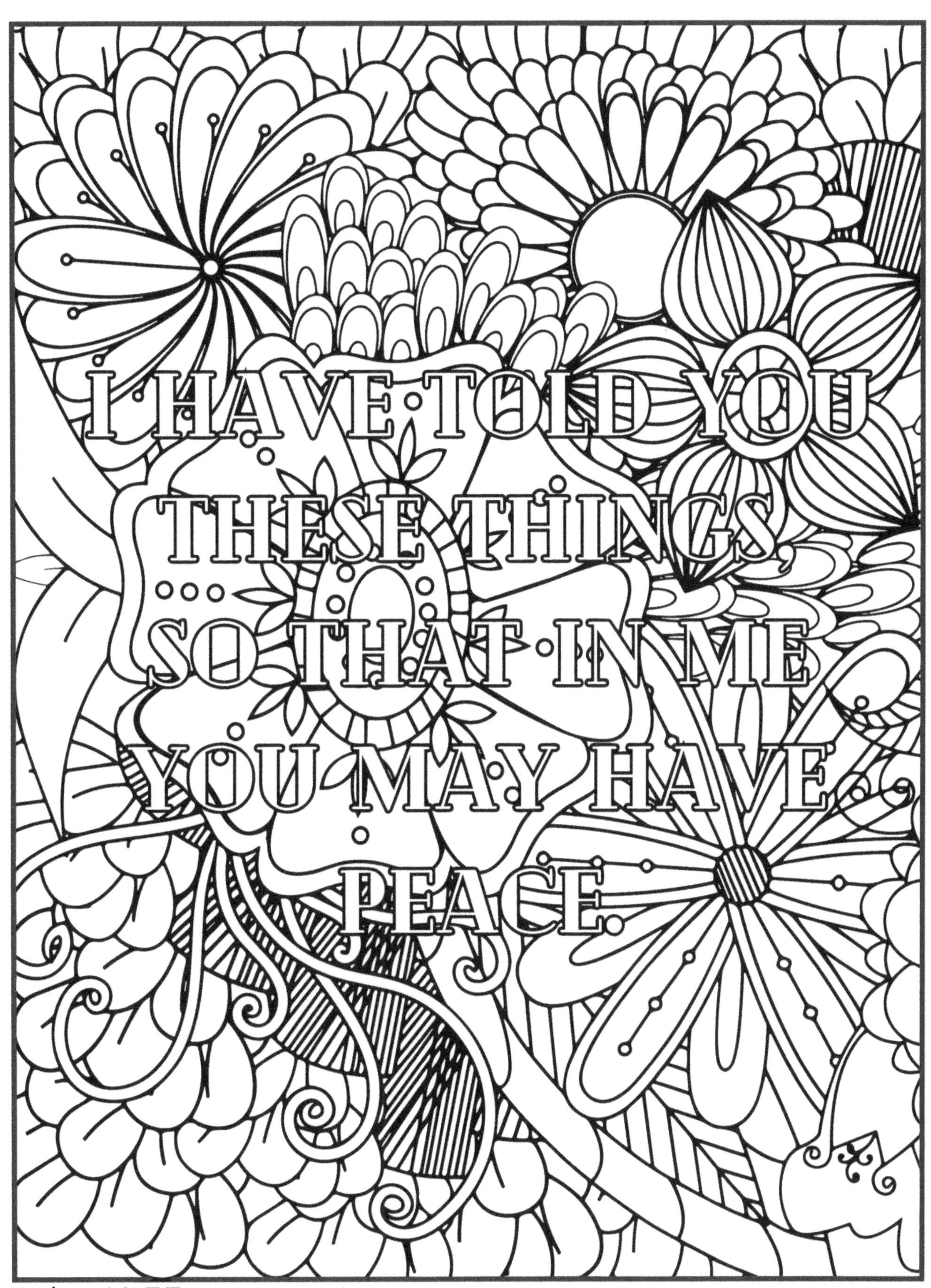

John 16:33

Scripture in Flowers

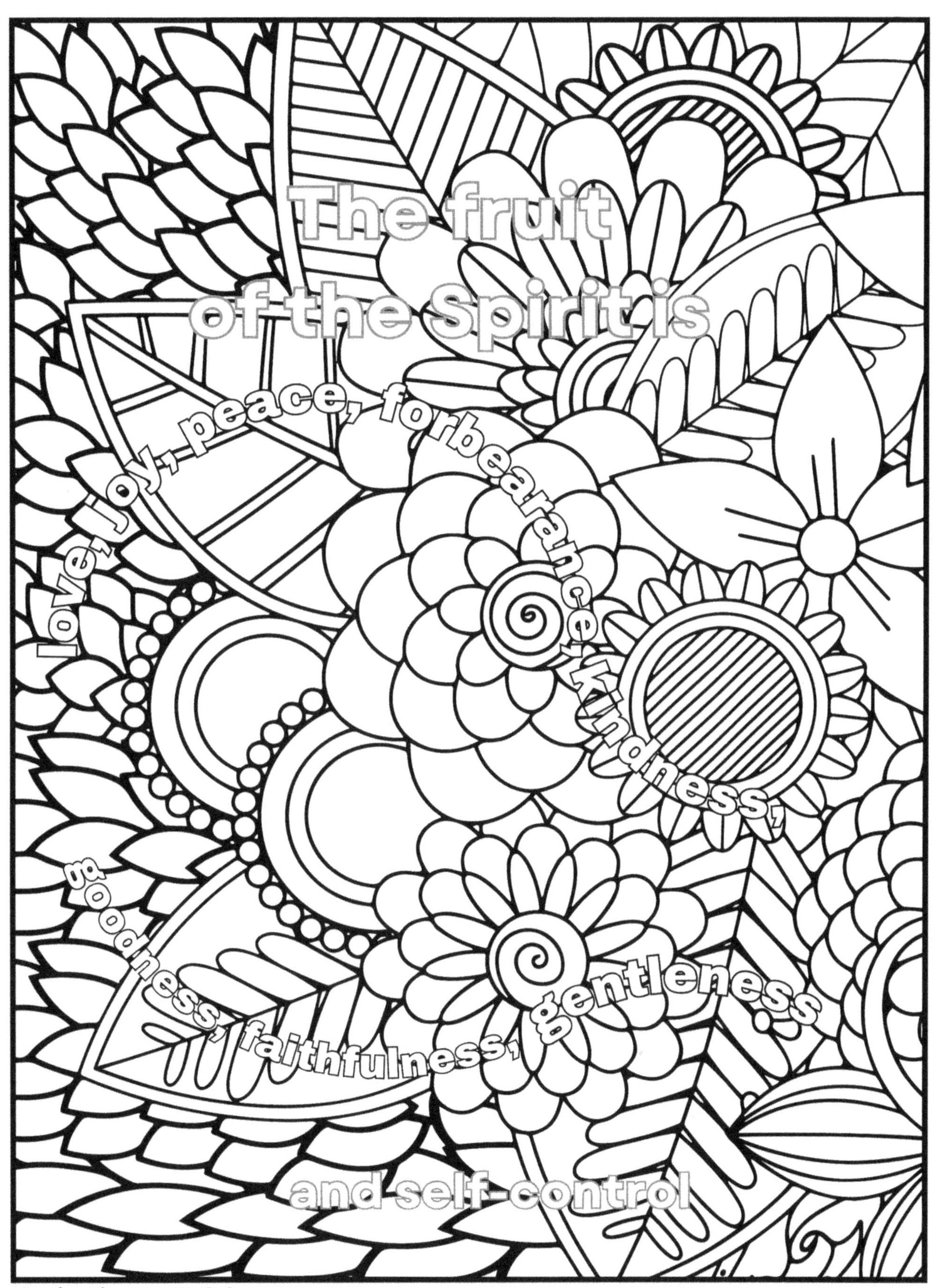

Galatians 5:22

Scripture in Flowers

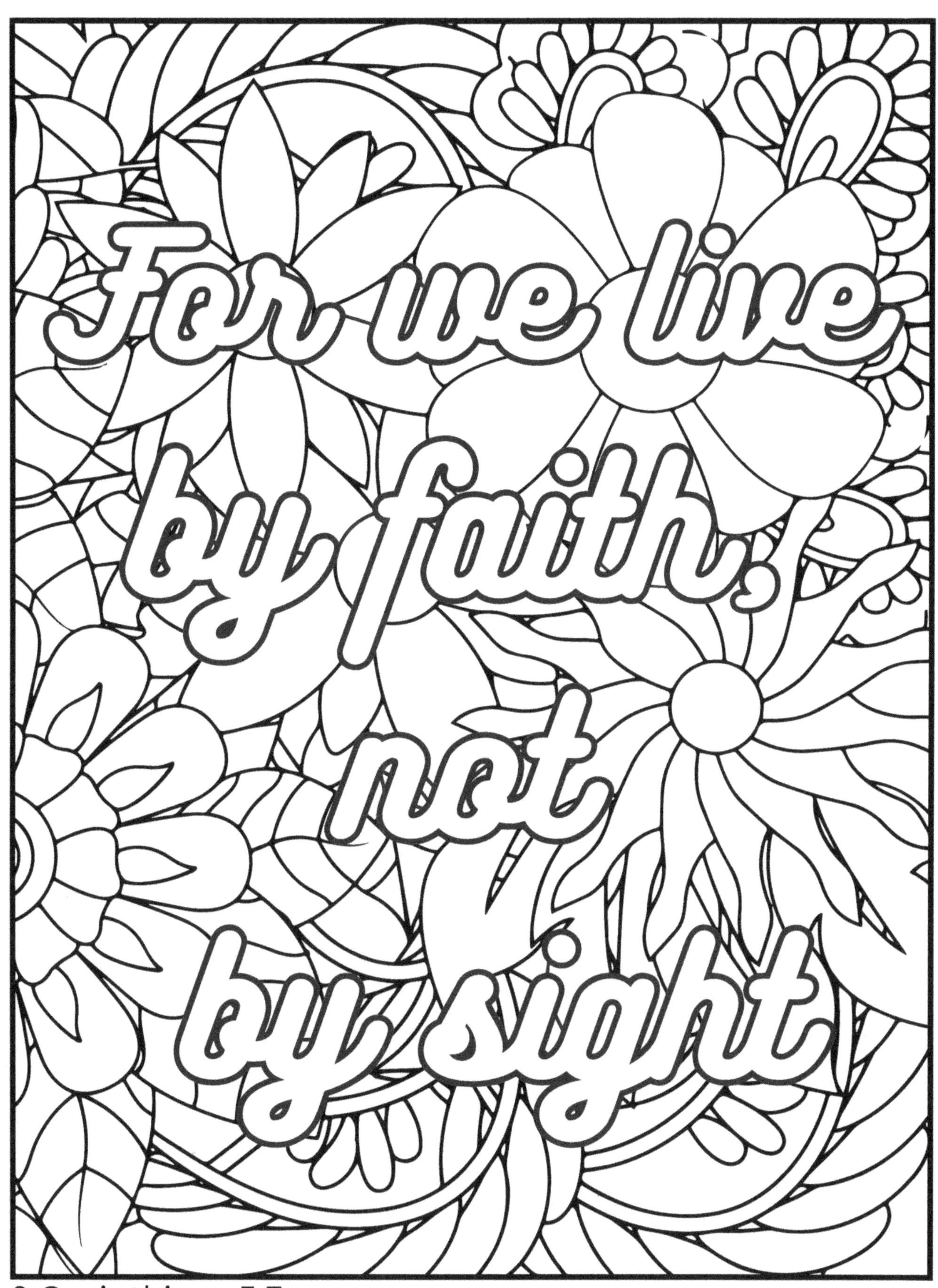

2 Corinthians 5:7

Scripture in
Flowers

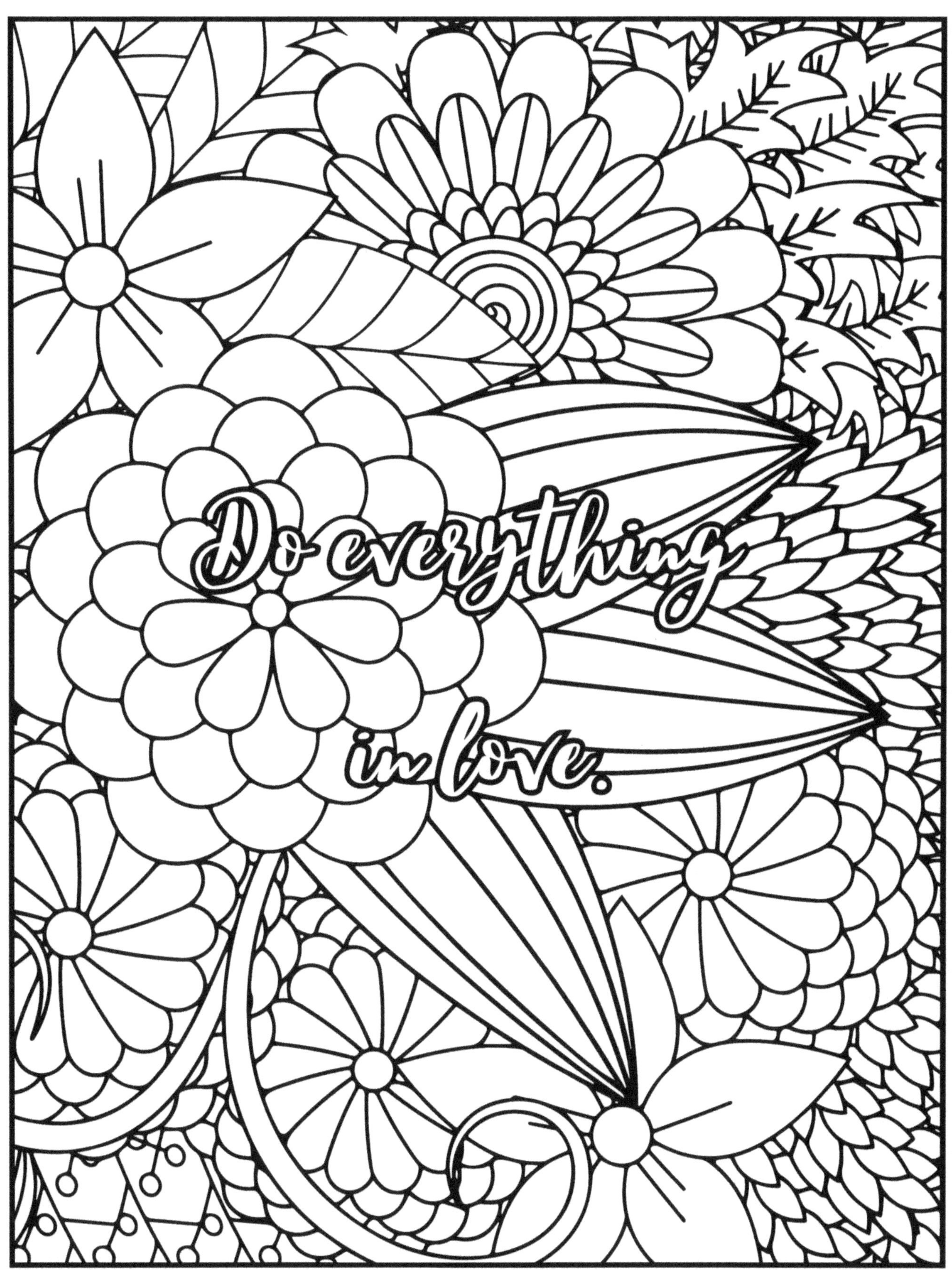

1 Corinthians 16:14

Scripture in
Flowers

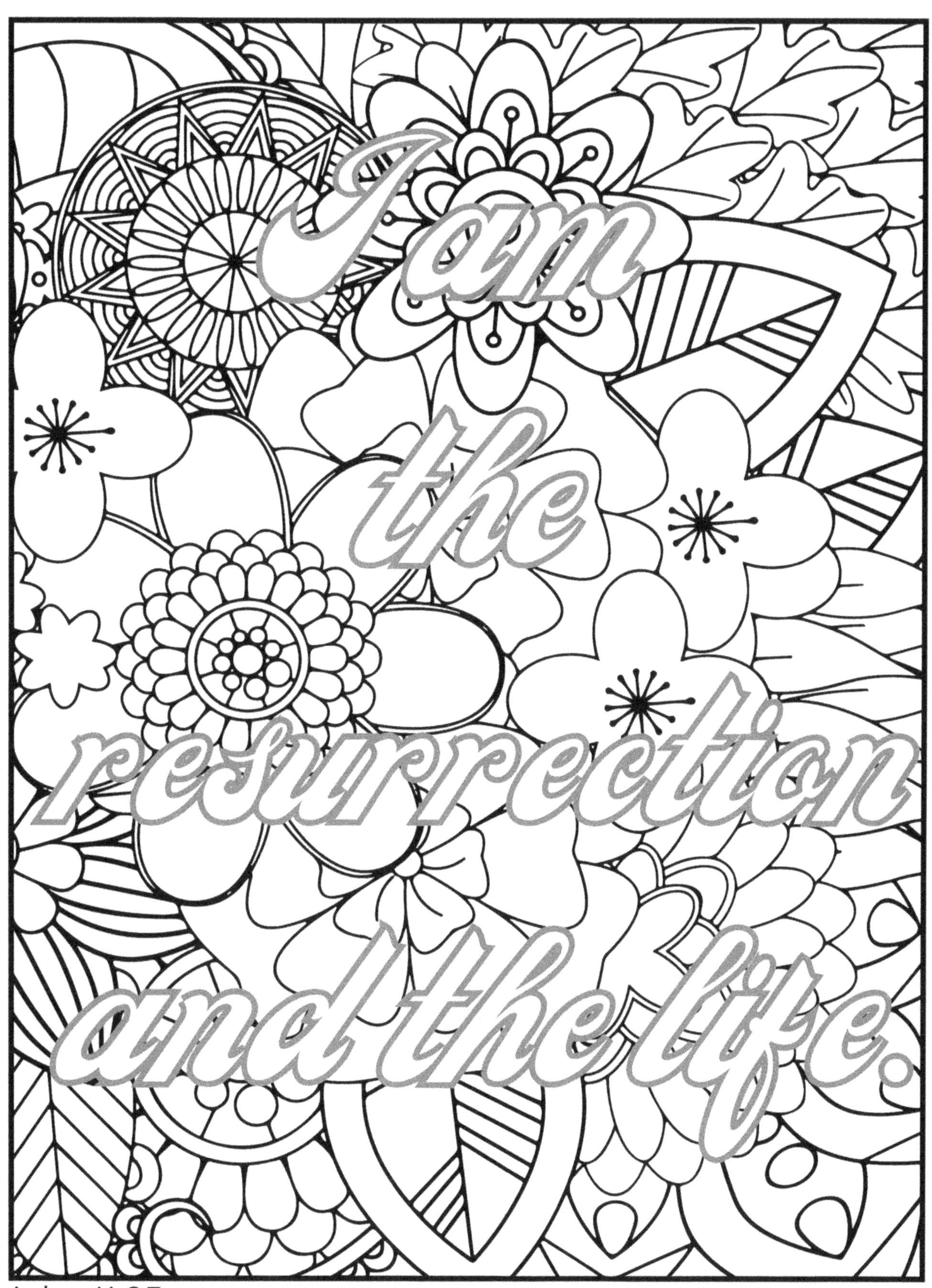

John 11:25

Scripture in Flowers

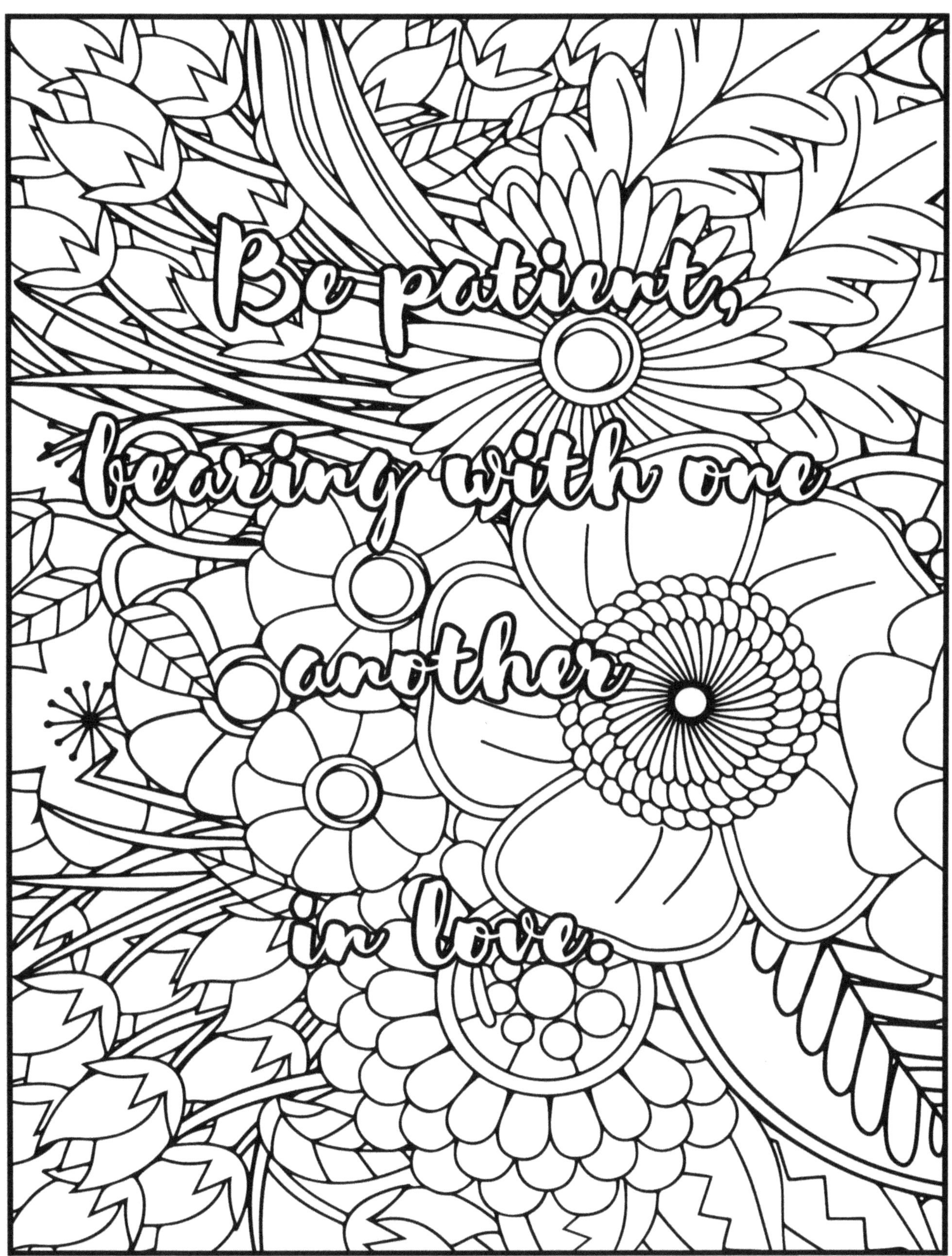

Ephesians 4:2

Scripture in
Flowers

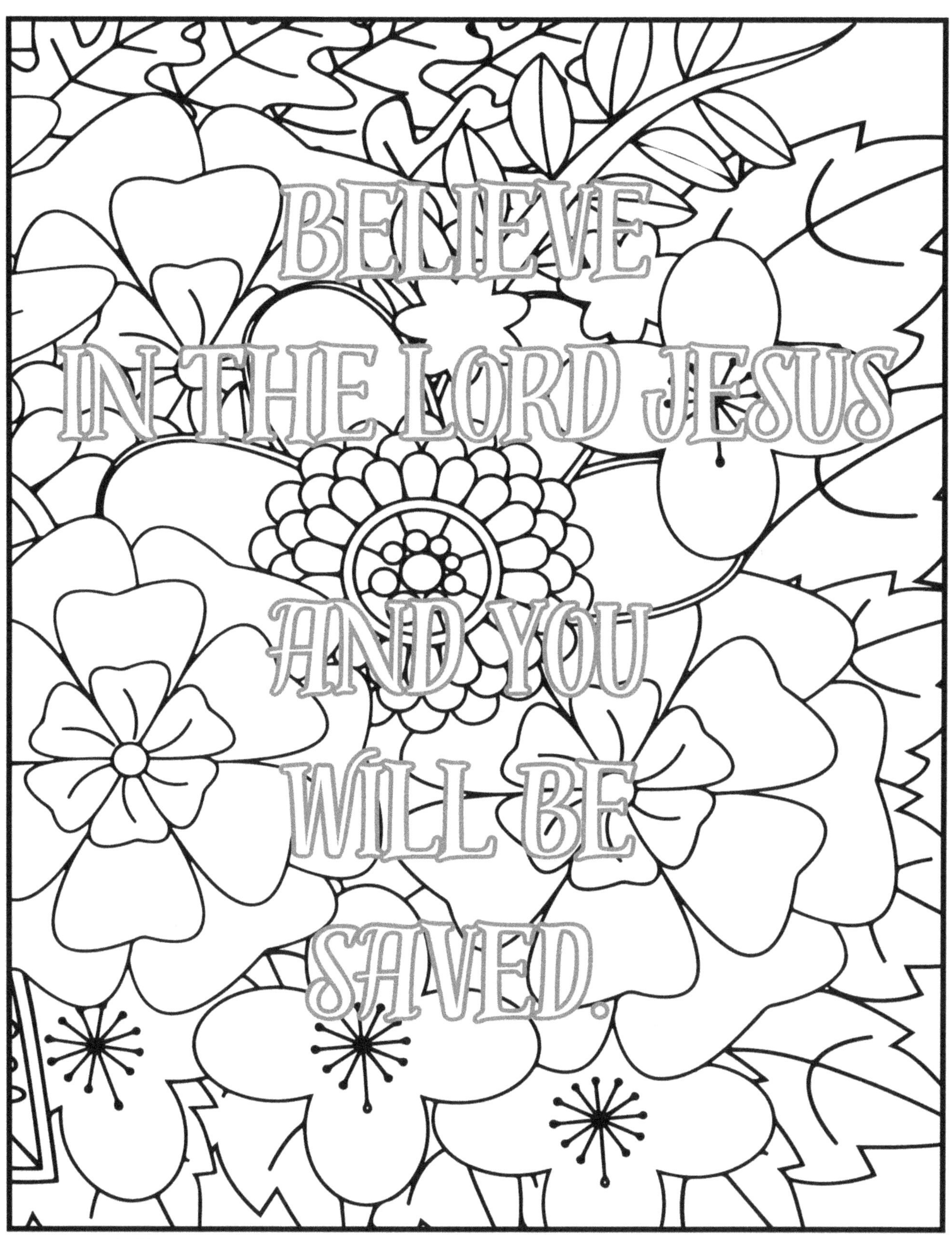

Acts 16:31

Scripture in Flowers

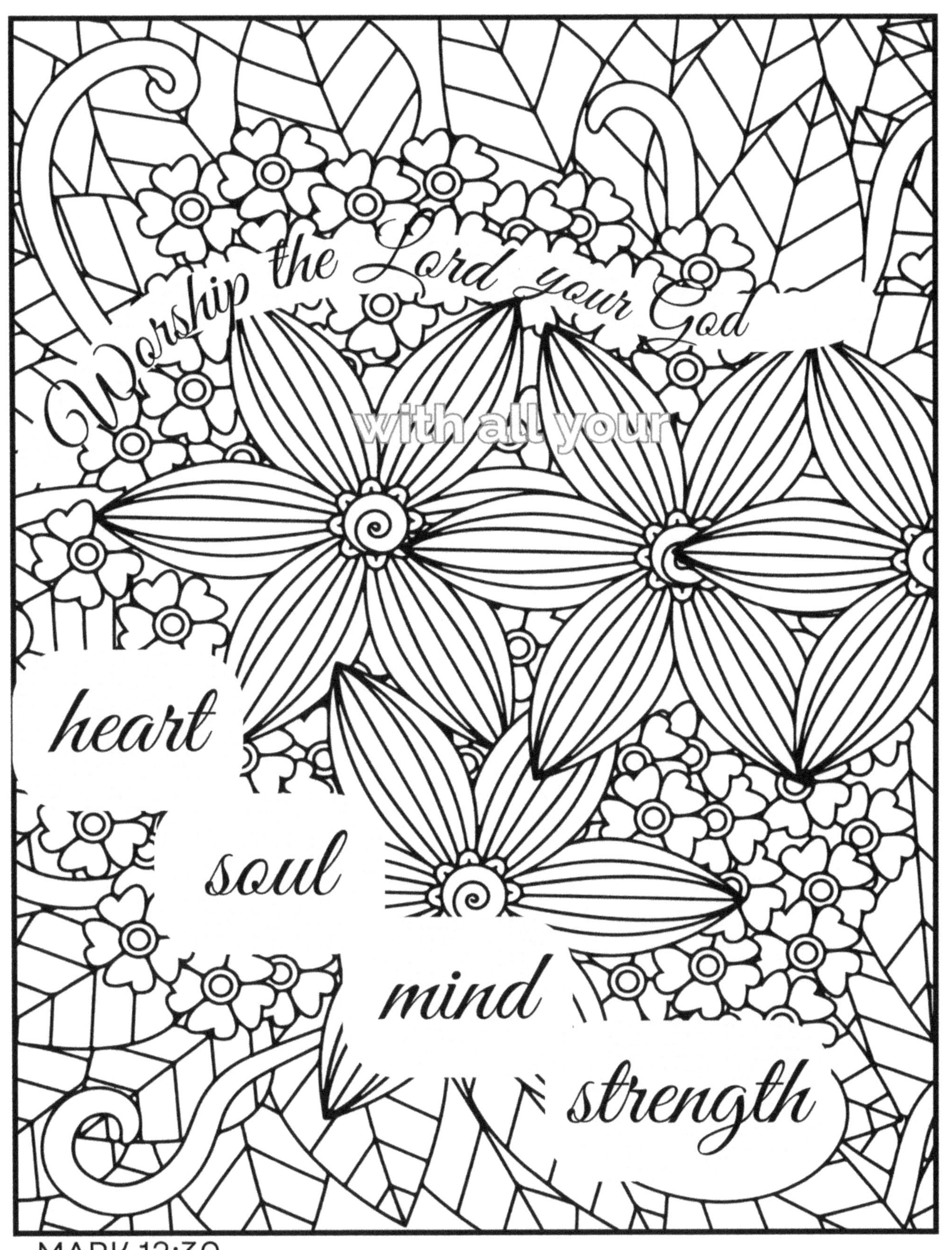

Worship the Lord your God
with all your
heart
soul
mind
strength
MARK 12:30

Scripture in
Flowers

Thank you for purchasing our coloring book. We appreciate your time. If you would, please take a moment to leave a review where you bought the book so that others hear about it, too. Reader reviews are so very important to writers. Thank you!

Contact us at hello@finchhollowpress.com

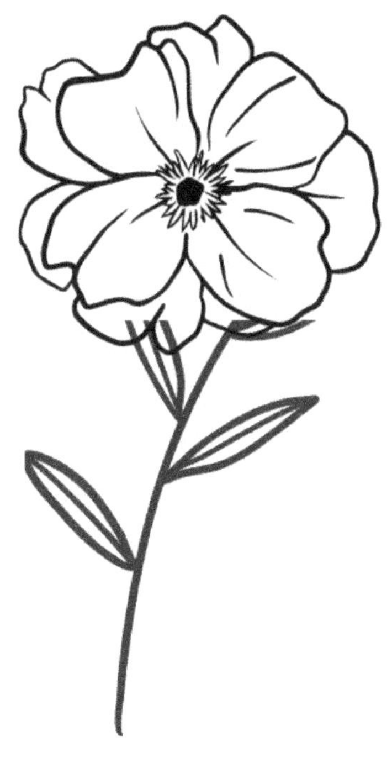